ROBBIE
A LIFE LESS ORDINARY

ROBBIE
A LIFE LESS ORDINARY

EMILY HERBERT

JOHN BLAKE

Published by John Blake Publishing Ltd,
3, Bramber Court, 2 Bramber Road,
London W14 9PB, England

www.blake.co.uk

This edition first published in hardback in 2006

ISBN 1 84454 232 7

British Library Cataloguing-in-Publication Data:

A catalogue record for this book is available from the British Library.

Design by www.envydesign.co.uk

Printed in Great Britain by Creative Print & Design, Wales.

1 3 5 7 9 10 8 6 4 2

Papers used by John Blake Publishing are natural, recyclable products made
from wood grown in sustainable forests. The manufacturing processes conform
to the environmental regulations of the country of origin.

Pictures reproduced by kind permission of Express Newspapers, Rex Features.

Every attempt has been made to contact the relevant copyright holders,
but some were unobtainable. We would be grateful if the appropriate people
could contact us.

CONTENTS

With thanks to
Dominique Ayling, Jane Sherwoord
and, as ever, Chris Williams

1

LUCKY FOR SOME

It was a bitterly cold night in February. Outside, the ground sparkled with frost and in the air there was a hint of the snow to come. Birds shivered in the trees, while the residents of Burslem, a small town in Stoke-on-Trent, huddled by their fires, safe from the cold outside. But in the Red Lion, a popular pub in the middle of Burslem, the atmosphere was warm enough to melt an iceberg: Jan Williams, the pub's landlady, had gone into labour and was giving birth to her second child at the nearby Royal Infirmary. Her husband, Peter, the pub landlord, was as excited as his wife.

Word soon spread. 'It's a boy!' cried the locals, before lifting their pints to toast the new arrival. The date was 13 February 1974, and one Robert Peter Maximillian Williams had made his way into the world. The family was jubilant. Jan already had an eight-year-old daughter, Sally, from a previous relationship; it seemed Robbie's arrival would make the family's happiness complete.

But while it was happy on the surface, Robbie's childhood was not all it seemed. Well liked right from the start, wherever he went, Robbie nonetheless remains haunted by shadows that first fell across his path very early in life. His well-documented drink and drug binges, his moodiness and depressions, and his seeming inability to build a lasting relationship can all be traced back to when he was a child. A chubby little boy who was self-conscious about his weight; a good Catholic boy with ambivalent feelings both towards women and his own sexuality; and, above all, the child of a single mother, who would go for years without seeing his first and greatest hero – his father.

Right from the start, Robbie was an exceptionally lively little boy, singing, dancing and showing off to the Red Lion's regulars. They were all enchanted by the performing toddler and he, in turn, lapped up the applause. 'Rob used to come down after closing time in his pyjamas and would sing a song or do impressions,' said his father Peter. 'He would be doing Margaret Thatcher or Brian Clough. They loved it.'

And he certainly had nerve. Years later, Robbie told the writer Mark McCrum that he entered himself in a talent competition – at the age of three. 'There was no pushy mother there,' he said, 'no parental supervision. My mum was actually shitting herself because she couldn't find me. It was just like, "There is the stage, I should be on that, because I'm good at that."' He won.

Robbie's birth three years earlier was not all the Williams family had to celebrate that year. A few months later, Peter won a pub comedy competition. The prize was £2 – followed by coming first on *New Faces* on television, for which he earned £5. Initially the family was jubilant, but Peter's success was to lead to hard times, in material terms at least. For, when Robbie was just two, his father left the family home to work as an entertainer, under the name Pete Conway. Jan was left to look after the pub on her own, while the marriage broke down irretrievably.

Robbie maintains that his parents' divorce did not harm him. 'Dad left when I was two,' he said years later. 'We've become mates now, but there's that blood link. My dad is very good at what he does. He's got excellent comic timing. He's so professional. That's what I admire him for. I was too young at the time to remember my parents' divorce. I can't wish for anything more than what I've got with my mum and sister; what I've got is fantastic. So I can't say I missed having a father full time. I mean, that's the way I grew up.' On other occasions, though, he was less sure. 'It must have had an effect, but my childhood was a very normal childhood,' he once said. 'It wasn't outrageous. I wasn't growing up sulking or becoming a Morrissey.' Perhaps not, but his father's long absences did have a profound effect on him, which haunts him to this day.

To a certain extent his grandfather stepped into the breach. Robbie once recalled, 'jumping up and down on the bed with my granddad, Jack Farrell, to strengthen me legs. He was in the army, a big man, Jack the Giant Killer, and he didn't want me growing up soft – so he'd get me to practise hitting him. I must have been three or four.'

Robbie, Jan and Sally, who he often refers to as his second mother, have always been remarkably close. Jan's mother Nan – real name Bertha – was also part of the family set-up. That was just as well, as far as Robbie was concerned, for a wild streak was also coming to the fore. The young Robert once threw the pub's £3,000 takings out of the window on a Port Vale FC match day – still his favourite team – followed by his mother's bra and his sister's knickers. History does not record the parental reaction.

And that urge to perform was becoming increasingly obvious. When Robbie was four, he was taken on holiday to Torremolinos. Halfway through the trip, Robbie wandered off and lost his mother in the crowds. She found him hours later, singing and dancing for a group of British tourists – with a busker's hat in front of him, to collect loose change.

A teacher at Robbie's primary school, John Collis, cast a young Robbie in his first play – as the devil. He recalled: 'It was certainly suiting to his personality at the time, and probably now as well. I can still see him now with those little red horns on.' He remembers Robbie as a fun child who had his fair share of mischief.

But, despite the relatively sunny skies of Robbie's early childhood, there were dark clouds forming on the horizon. His adult life has been troubled by demons, some of which began to take shape early on. Robbie's weight has fluctuated alarmingly as an adult, and he has been the first to admit that he suffered from eating disorders in the past. The seeds of his problems were sown back then. 'I've had a problem with my weight ever since I could remember,' he said in an interview some years ago.

'My first memory is of two little boys laughing at my belly on the beach [at Babbacombe]. In Take That I jumped around so much I could have eaten what I liked, but I still starved and binged. My mum would worry about me being so thin and I'd think I was fat.' Teenage girls, it would seem, are not the only ones plagued by body dysmorphia, the illness that means you cannot see your body in its true shape. And it was a subject he brought up repeatedly, adding at one point, 'I really was a little chubby thing.'

Another early memory, he said, 'is of being on my Uncle Don's shoulders, marching through London shouting, "Maggie Maggie Maggie – Out Out Out." Great lyrics, them. I'd never vote Tory – I know what they've done to this country. Besides, I live in Stoke. You just can't get away with that kind of stuff there.'

Locals remember him fondly. One person who saw a great deal of him was hairdresser Patricia McNair, who was friends with Jan and who had a young son, Jamie, with whom Robbie used to play. She also used to cut Robbie's hair at her salon, Patricia's. 'He used to come over on Saturday night and entertain us with his songs and dances,' she said. 'Even then, when he was just seven, you could see he was an entertainer. He was a great kid – naughty and lots of fun.'

Some people might say that Robbie's character never really changed from those very young days. Unusually for a rock star, his fan base spreads from toddlers to grannies, from teenage girls to Robbie wannabes. And that may well be down not only to his undoubted charisma, but also to the fact that, just as he did back then, he shows his vulnerability and wears his heart on his sleeve. To this day, his performances contain an element of clowning around, mixed with a boyish desire to be the centre of attention. As a child, Robbie was a natural entertainer; as an entertainer, Robbie still retains something of the child.

Another element Robbie carries with him from his childhood is Catholic guilt. As an adult, he famously had a statue of St Teresa at the end of his bed in his Notting Hill home, a present from his very Catholic mother. This statue, claimed Robbie, stood in judgement on his behaviour. 'When I come home drunk,' he once remarked, 'St Teresa turns her head away from me, I swear she does.' It might have been a joke, but his religious beliefs are serious enough – so much so that they continue to disturb him when he feels he has misbehaved.

His Catholic background has stayed with him in other ways, as well. Asked once if he enjoyed pornography, Robbie replied, 'No. There's something wrong about it. I always get these voices inside my head saying, "That's someone's daughter." It's not my voice, either. And that's as far as I am going with that answer.'

However, those problems were all very much in the future, as the miniature Robbie clowned his way around the world. He was also introduced to live music for the first time, as he revealed when asked about the first gig he ever attended.

'Showaddywaddy, when I was seven. It was at the Queen's Hall in Burslem and me mum used to run the Red Lion pub round the corner. It was fantastic. Well, as much as I can remember. I wanted the Teddy Boy outfit and everything but me mum wouldn't get me one because she thought I'd grow out of it.'

He found some unusual fans, in one case an international statesman. When he was eight, Jan took Robbie on holiday to the Victoria Falls Hotel in Zimbabwe, where they saw Joshua Nkomo, the country's president. 'I said to my mum, "That's the president of Africa,"' said Robbie. 'It was the time Lenny Henry was doing his African impressions and I went up to Joshua Nkomo when my mum wasn't looking and I said, "Hello, I'm Robert from England and I can do impressions of black men." And then I did my Lenny Henry. He just laughed, and then I had a great chat with him. He was fascinated that a kid could just come up to him when he had these men with guns – a kid who was not scared. He signed an autograph for me.'

There was, according to Robbie, a very good reason for being in Zimbabwe. 'Me mum's a white witch! She reads Tarot cards, she reads palms. She actually went to a witch doctor in Victoria Falls in Africa and he read the bones for her. I do believe in it because, once, I had my fortune told in this gypsy camp and I can't tell you what she said but it was amazingly accurate. I know a lot of people told my mum I was going to be famous, but she didn't tell me.'

However, there were problems growing on the home front. Jan never enjoyed running the pub on her own after Pete left, and soon takings began to fall. The business was suffering, although, ironically, this led indirectly to Robbie channeling his talents properly for the first time. The family moved out of the pub and, after a short spell on a council estate, into a semi in the nearby town of Tunstall. 'I used to say we had it tough, which made my mum upset because it wasn't true,' said Robbie, after he became famous. 'There's always that wanting to be someone else or feeling guilty about everything you've been given. People only get into this game because they have something to prove, so you're dealing with a bunch of really insecure people who need to be loved. Don't get me wrong, I can be rude if you're rude to me, but I'm very polite. I remember as a kid, if you opened a door to a lady, she'd like you.'

Jan was now running a florist's, while Robbie attended Mill Hill Primary School, where he promptly blossomed – in extra curricular activities, at least. Robbie took part in school plays, appeared in children's fashion shows and joined a number of amateur dramatic associations, including the Stoke-on-Trent Operatic Society, the Newcastle Amateur Dramatic Society and the Stoke-on-Trent Pantomime Society. Within a couple of years he graduated to greater heights still: aged 11, he was taking part in Hans Christian Andersen productions, playing the king's son in *The King and I* and was the fiddler in *Fiddler on the Roof*. He was known as Swellhead. But those weight problems were ever present: fellow pupils also called him Fatsikins, a jibe he deflected by making them laugh.

He was also beginning to show signs of the ambition that would take him to the very top of the pop world. Robbie may have a happy-go-lucky air about him, but no one signs one of the world's biggest record deals without a certain degree of steel. And so it is with Robbie. 'Do you know what? When I was a child, I told my Nan I didn't know what I was gonna do, but, when I was 12, I told her I'd be a millionaire by the time I was 22 and I was!' he said shortly after leaving Take That. 'And I had no doubt in my mind that I was gonna do it and I also have no doubt now that I'm gonna carry on and I'm gonna be a huge star again.'

In those early years, though, being a pop star was not necessarily on the agenda. 'I remember watching TV when I was young and Kajagoogoo came on,' he said. 'My mum said, "I bet you'd like to be a pop star just like them." She was quite taken aback when I told her being a pop star didn't interest me at all – what I wanted to be more than anything else was an actor.'

It was when he was in his early teens that Robbie began to see his father once more. Peter, a policeman and electricity inspector before he became a publican and then a comedian, was a hero to his son – which might go a long way towards explaining some of the darker sides of Robbie's character. To this day, Robbie rarely talks about him, but it is always telling when he does. When asked why he started bingeing on drink and drugs as an adult, Robbie once replied, 'What do they expect me to say, that maybe my dad didn't love me enough?' Strangely, the first time Robbie ever got drunk was when, as a 13-year-old, he visited Peter in Scarborough, where he was working as a comedian.

But the plain fact of the matter was that Peter just was not there during Robbie's early childhood. 'Rob is sensitive about Pete,' said Tony Hollins, Peter's best man and later manager, 'because he doesn't want the public to know that there were a great many years when they simply weren't in contact at all.' When they did meet again, Robbie 'came to idolise his father', according to Hollins, but 'he realised that his mother had been left with the responsibility of looking after the family on her own'.

But the new father-son relationship now flourished.

Robbie began to see Peter much more and was influenced by his father's choice of music. Pete was a great aficionado of the likes of Frank Sinatra and Ella Fitzgerald, and would play them to his son. Then, once a week, the two would visit The Duke William pub in Hanley, where they would take to the stage on open-mike night.

'He thinks he was just an average boy from Stoke, but he was more talented than that,' said Peter. 'He always loved the stage. When he left school he stood up in front of everyone and sang "Every Time We Say Goodbye", the Cole Porter song. Robbie has sung that song since he was a kid and has recorded it himself. He grew up with Sinatra and Dean Martin and Nat King Cole because I was very much into them myself – still am!'

Robbie himself credits his father with being the man who gave him an abiding love for the stage. 'I've got a sense of showbiz from my dad, but it's never going to be the same act,' he once said. 'He's an old-school comedian.' And his tastes were also being formed elsewhere. 'I have ridiculously eclectic tastes,' he said after the release of 'Angels'. 'The first album I bought was Pink Floyd's *The Wall*. I grew up listening to Showaddywaddy, Adam and the Ants, Darts and loads of electric stuff – Doug E Fresh and the Get Fresh Crew, Afrika Bambaataa, Grandmaster Melle Mel & the Furious Five. At school I listened to hip hop, but I aspire to Las Vegas. Fifteen years from now, I just want to be able to sing "Angels" and say, "This song has been very good to me." Tom Jones is a definite hero.'

Robbie's father helped the aspiring youngster find his first job at a local radio station by introducing him to one of his DJ friends. Robbie helped collate the sports news on a Saturday and would sometimes come in during the week to do impressions for one of the afternoon shows, all for just £10 a week.

But even then there was a competitive edge to the relationship between father and son, as Peter attempted to show Robbie that success in life had to be fought for. One way of doing this was to play games with his son – and beat him every time. Some years ago, Peter explained that he never let Robbie win anything as a boy, as a way of explaining how the lesson was taught – but, of course, Robbie took a different view of it. 'You know,' he said in 2002, 'I suppose it served me well. But I wish he'd just have let me win a few games when I was a kid. One game of pool, you know? One game of table tennis.'

By this time, Pete was dividing his time between the northern club circuit and summer holiday camps. As their relationship developed anew, Robbie would go and spend three weeks with him every summer at camps in Scarborough, Cornwall or Wales, where he would pick up the tricks of the trade. 'He's very funny, my dad,' said Robbie. 'I used to piss myself laughing when I watched his act, even though I knew all the punchlines. He's a pro's pro. I've got a lot of respect for him. There's loads of stuff I remember learning from him then – like his mike technique. I used to watch *New Faces* on the telly with him, and he'd say to the contestants, "Open your eyes, son – let 'em in." I still remember that today when I'm on stage.'

It certainly sealed his fate. After finally spending time with a father he idolised, it was almost inevitable that Robbie would end up in showbusiness – and in a cheeky chappy persona, at that. 'I grew up on holiday camps. I grew up with very old-school entertainers – their profession was to entertain people,' he said. 'Their expression, as they came on stage, it was, "Always remember to smile." That was a sign on the door as you went to go up on stage. "Always remember to smile, 'cause they smile with you." Now it seems that there's a sign on the door saying, "Always look at your feet, because if you look at the crowd, you might get scared and you might scare them too."'

By this time Robbie had moved on to St Margaret Ward RC High School, where he did not prove himself academically. Sports were his forte; sums were not. But, likeable and lively as ever, Robbie quickly became popular and, of course, the class clown. 'I was just the chubby boy who would go around pulling faces and telling jokes and I found myself with a big circle of friends,' he said.

The authority figures at the time remember a naughty Robbie. 'We called him Robert or Williams when he was in trouble,' said deputy head Frank Jevons, rather tellingly. Robbie never made it to the school's Board of Honours, situated in the entrance hall, but there were compensations – the school also has a display board for newspaper cuttings featuring old pupils. It is fair to say that Robbie made his mark there. He himself puts it all behind him now. 'It sounds strange, but I can't draw on any of the experiences I had in school because it's gone for me,' he once said. 'It's really sad. I had a fantastic time at school, we had the best laugh I've ever had, but I can't really recall any of those feelings because that person's dead.'

At this point, sport featured very largely in his life. Robbie recalls sticking pictures from *Shoot* and *Match* on his bedroom walls – 'The whole Oxford United team had one bollock hanging out, that was my favourite' – and made it to become the Burslem Golf Club junior captain of fifteen. Funnily enough, though, Robbie does harbour some regrets. 'I wish I'd worked harder at school,' he said back in 1994. 'Even though I hated the lessons, I loved school. I used to go for a laugh because I had such fun and I went to learn about life, not what "x" equals.'

Robbie was very much the clown, never the lothario. 'I guess I was the classic case at school,' he said on another occasion. 'If I couldn't get noticed for my body or my looks, the only thing left was to make people laugh. Me and my schoolmates, Peter O'Reilly and Richard Cook, formed a gang and we became the classroom idiots. I only went to school to have a laugh during the breaks. Walking home together afterwards was a great lark, too. We were always playing daft pranks. But we ended up living up to our name of the class idiot with all the exam results we didn't get. I don't regret any of it. I always thought lessons were a bind. And in the meantime I was still working away at scoring with the girls.'

For all his subsequent reputation as a ladies' man, little Robbie – Fatsikins – did not have much success with girls. 'I went through school just wanting girls to like me and fancy me. But mainly they didn't,' he said. 'When I was about nine, this bloke at school told me there were loads of different ways to kiss a girl. I was disgusted. It didn't seem right or proper. I remember saying, "There's no way you can kiss a girl like you're telling me, mate." But, as soon as his back was turned, I started practising air kissing. I was obsessed with it for months. In fact, from that day on I have tried to snog anything with a pulse.'

He succeeded relatively early on. 'I was really into girls by primary school stage,' he once said. 'All the others were playing on their computers and I'd be snogging whoever I could get. I had my first proper French kiss at 10.' Three years later he had his first proper date: he took a young friend out to see the film *Three Men and a Baby*.

It was a year later, aged 14, that Robbie lost his virginity. He told the tale himself, with all the clowning and self-deprecation that became his trademark.

He later recalled, 'She was tall, red-haired and mad for it. She came up to me in the classroom one day and in front of all my mates said, "Your place, Friday, after school."

'Of course I put on a big, macho show as if to say, "Of course, I've done this dozens of times." But, although I fancied her, this girl scared the life out of me. On the Friday I took her home and, after a quick snog, completely lost my bottle. But, as I asked her to leave, I suddenly realised how much stick I was going to get from my friends. I took her up to my room and, about two and a half minutes later, it was all over. It was a less than impressive performance, but I was thrilled and naturally told all my friends what a stud I'd been.' Whatever he might have thought about himself, Robbie was obviously something of a charmer even then.

Clearly Robbie remembers the school with a degree of fondness. In April 2001, he contributed some items, including the handwritten lyrics to his song 'Angels' and his bed, to the charity auction Give It Sum, which Robbie himself established. The auction raised £138,900 – including £27,000 for the lyrics and £13,000 for the bed – while Robbie enthused about where some of the money should go. The recipient-to-be was none other than his old school. 'I'm building a new art and drama wing on my old wing, the Robbie Williams wing, which is amazing,' he said at the time. 'It's what you dream of – I'm doing everything I've ever dreamed of doing and I'm only 27.'

Back when he was only 15, Robbie was proving himself an extremely talented actor, so much so that he landed the role of the Artful Dodger in the North Staffordshire Amateur Operatic Society's production of *Oliver!*. He proceeded to indulge in some method acting. 'When we were rehearsing, we got a professional pickpocket to show us how it should be done,' said Brian Rawlins, who was the founder of the society and who played Fagin. 'Robbie became very good at it. You would keep finding things missing in rehearsals and then Robbie would pop up waving your wallet or whatever he had taken.

'Robbie was a nice kid with lots of personality, and confident even then. He was very much the local boy with a very strong local accent, which he had to cover up when he played Dodger. His mum was great too – they were very close. He helped every Saturday afternoon in the flower shop she owned in Newcastle-under-Lyme. I remember bumping into them the day before he went for the Take That audition. Robbie was really nervous but his mum always thought he would do it.'

Brian remains fond of his young protégé. 'He was a bright lad with a spark in his eye which still comes across now, but he was also very sensitive,' he said. 'He would get upset if he was ever told off and would get quite emotional about it. I suppose you could say that he seems to have lost that sensitivity now, but underneath all the bravado I would like to think he is still that sensitive lad I used to know. He has had his problems, which have been well documented in the press, and I remember that things would always touch him quite deeply, so I guess that could be one of the triggers to his problems.

'I'm not a big fan of his music but there's no doubt that he's very talented and I see no reason why he won't eventually crack America. I used to be in the PR business and in my opinion he just needs to market himself differently in the US. At the moment he's seen as a very English lad, but he needs to forget that and become more international. He should change his public persona.

'I haven't seen him for years. The last time I saw him was while he was in Take That. He was the only one out of that group who had anything about him and it was obvious he would be the most successful. He had that amazing spark and energy. By comparison the others were all really weak. Everyone in the society follows his career and we all wish him well.'

For Robbie, the role of the Artful Dodger marked something of a turning point in his life. 'It was my first lead role,' he told Mark McCrum. 'And I walked out from the side of the stage, whistling and doing this walk, and the whole audience just took a breath, gasped. I physically heard them do it. I'd just won them over by walking on stage. And I can always remember coming out for the curtain call and my cheers drowning everyone else's out. I thought, I really am good at this.'

It was to be a momentous year for Robbie. First, there was terrible grief as Robbie's aunt died, causing dreadful upset to him and his family. 'My auntie Jo died of cancer when I was 15,' he recalled some years later. 'I knew she was ill, but I didn't know she was going to die. I loved her. It still upsets me. I knew I had to be strong for my mum. I can remember the funeral: I didn't cry but then everyone left to go to the wake and I just stayed at the grave and broke down in tears. I cried and cried and cried. I sobbed my heart out. After that, I didn't cry about it again.'

More upheaval was to come. As Robbie approached his exams, Jan was also beginning to think about her talented but unacademic son's future and it had nothing to do with GSCEs. Jan had turned on the radio to hear the entrepreneur Nigel Martin-Smith talking about forming a new boy band, one to rival the massively popular US outfit New Kids On The Block. And so, pretending to be Robbie, Jan wrote a letter to Martin-Smith asking for an audition, which duly came about. Robbie performed well, but Martin-Smith was not yet quite convinced. He then wrote to Jan, asking for something to corroborate the audition. Jan duly replied with copies of local press cuttings, talking about Robbie as 'an uncanny stage presence'.

Robbie sat his GCSEs and a couple of months later learned he had failed the lot. This was not altogether surprising, as Robbie's exam techniques left a great deal to be desired. He later admitted to having taken acid for the first time half an hour before his RE GCSE. 'I knew I hadn't a hope in hell of passing it, so I thought, This is a laugh. How can I make it even more of one? I was tripping all the way through. It was great! "Why was Jesus refused entry into Nazareth?" Because he wasn't wearing a shirt and tie. "What did Peter say when he was baptised?" Glug glug. I realise now this was a very bad idea.'

The day Robbie found out his results was to prove the most momentous one yet. 'The day I was told I was in the band, me and my friend Lee just got our exam results and we both failed really badly,' Robbie recalled. 'We didn't know how we were going to tell our parents. So we went to the bottle shop and bought ten each of the cheapest cans of bitters we could buy and sat on the bowling green and just necked these bitters – trying to figure out a way to tell our parents, because they had hoped so much for us. They wanted me to go on to university. I went back to my mum pissed and said that I had something to tell her and she said she had something to tell me – "You're in the band." Then she said, "What did you have to tell me?" and I said it didn't matter. I ran upstairs and shouted at the top of my voice, "I'm going to be famous!"'

He was right. Robbie Williams, superstar, was on his way.

2
I'M GOING TO
BE FAMOUS

As is so often the case, Robbie's inclusion in Take That was actually an afterthought. The band's manager, Nigel Martin-Smith, had originally only been looking for four boys and thought he had found them: Gary Barlow, the singer/songwriter; Mark Owen, the looker; and Jason Orange and Howard Donald, the dancers. Then, in early 1990, Jan had heard Martin-Smith on the radio and written that fateful letter and Robbie edged in after all. 'I originally wanted Take That to be a four-piece band,' Martin-Smith said some time later. 'The only reason I took on a fifth was because I thought one of them would be bound to drop out, get a job at Tesco's or get married.'

Nigel Martin-Smith, who discovered Robbie, left school at 15 with no qualifications – just like Robbie himself. In June 1981, he launched a modelling and casting agency, which by 1990 had grown to employ 10 staff and make a £1 million annual turnover. He had always been interested in pop music, though, and so jumped at the chance to put together a rival outfit to the massively successful US band New Kids On The Block. 'I'll just use my instincts,' he once said. 'They need no singing skills, but they must be able to move well and have that star quality. Yes, that's vital.' As for the name of the new band, it came from watching a Madonna video, in which she grabbed her crotch, thrust it towards the audience and shouted, 'Take that!'

There was initially some debate within Robbie's family as to whether he should actually take on the job. It is often forgotten now that Take That was originally formed to appeal to the gay circuit, and the atmosphere surrounding the band was very gay: Martin-Smith is gay; they were going to perform as five young boys pirouetting in gay clubs ('I didn't know that sort of thing happened,' Robbie said later) – and Robbie was only 15. But Pete was relaxed about it, pointing out that the showbusiness world is filled with gay men, while it was Robbie's grandmother who settled the argument. 'I'd be more worried if he was going to become a priest,' she said.

The group had come together slowly. At its heart was Gary Barlow, lead singer and songwriter and, much to Robbie's later fury, perceived to be the real talent in the band. Certainly, he had been in the music game for a very long time. 'I always loved music,' he said in an interview in 1991, 'and, when I was 10, I was given a choice of a BMX bike or a keyboard for Christmas. Within two weeks I'd done everything on the keyboard and Dad had to buy me a better one.' He didn't stop there, and within a year he was playing organ in a cabaret band 'where all the other members were at least 50'. Something of a child prodigy, when he was 16, he won the BBC's Carol for Christmas competition.

Gary and Mark met when Mark was barely into his teens, and together they formed a group called The Cutest Rush. 'I was fourteen,' said Mark in that same interview, 'looking for a work as a session singer and Gary was this genius keyboard player.' The two decided they had to find decent management and so went to Nigel Martin-Smith – who had been recommended by Gary's aunt.

Some years after they hit the big time, Barlow recalled exactly where he was when he heard from Martin-Smith: 'I was out the front, washing my car, a Ford Orion. You could fit the speaker for my keyboard in the back seat.' And Martin-Smith had 'an idea for a band ... the comradeship between five nice young people'. He showed Gary a video of New Kids On The Block, while Gary warned his new manager that he couldn't dance. Don't worry, said nice Nigel, you can be the singer in the middle and the others will work around you.

In one of those strange coincidences that litter the annals of showbiz history, Martin-Smith had just made the acquaintance of another two men — Jason and Howard. Jason had spent a year touring the clubs as a dancer in a TV show presented by Pete Waterman and Michela Strachan called *The Hit Man and Her*. 'It was like an apprenticeship,' he said. His friend Howard, meanwhile, had started dancing at 16, appearing in the J and D Dance Troupe. Howard signed up with Martin-Smith as a male model and formed a dance troupe with Jason, called Street Beat.

It was very successful. The two made the finals of *Come Dancing* three times, won twice and were placed second in the European championships and third in the world, with an eccentric dance version of *Seven Brides for Seven Brothers*. It was because of that background that the two had a strong say in the group's choreography. 'We all agreed on a sexy image, like the bare chests, coloured waistcoats and beads; but with the dancing, I try to keep it tight, so it appeals to both the older and the teenage market,' said Howard.

At first, it was just the four of them. Gary gave up the club jobs and sold his car. 'We all had jobs we jacked in,' he said later. 'Jason, painting and decorating; Howard, car spraying; Mark was a tea boy at Strawberry Studios. Our manager put us on a little wage and kept us all hyped up. I remember saying to Jason, "One day we're going to be coming in and talking to each other about the houses we've bought and the cars we've bought and the watches we've bought." We laugh about that moment, because that's exactly what we do.'

It was at that stage that Martin-Smith informed his new band that he was considering adding a new member. The foursome were shown a photograph. 'This picture looked like a 14-year-old school kid,' said Gary, and he wasn't far off. 'The manager said, "His name's Robbie and he's got a really good voice." He was one of those precocious school kids who danced outrageously and was dead cheeky but quite a likeable young lad.'

Martin-Smith was, in fact, extremely impressed with Robbie and, despite the later bitterness between the two, was generous in his praise. 'Robbie Williams is a huge talent, but his talent is not just for music,' he said years later. 'It's for playing the part of being a rock star. When he auditioned for me, he did impressions – and very good ones. I remember in the very early days of Take That we were in a karaoke bar and Robbie got up and sang "Mack The Knife". He could have been Frank Sinatra. He was amazing. I knew he had bags of talent. He only gave a bit away at the time. Robbie's someone who needs new challenges because he gets bored quickly. He's proved that he can be a solo star and he'll be looking for the next thing. I'm sure he could make it as an actor. I have no doubt about that.'

And so, contracts were signed in September 1990.

Robbie was off to join the band – and no one summed up his first impressions better than he did himself. 'I remember the first time I ever met the lads at the Take That auditions,' he said. 'I came with my mum and I was saying through the corner of my mouth, "Right, Mum – go now." Marky was doing exactly the same thing at the other end of the street with his mum.

'As I walked into the audition, there was this guy sat there with really untrendy Adidas bottoms on, massive Converse trainers, a stupid spiky haircut – and I'm not dissing him here, I mean it lovingly. He's got his legs crossed with his hands on his knee and this bloody leather briefcase, which had song sheets for crap cabaret songs in it. I looked at him and I was told, "This is Gary Barlow. He's a professional club singer and he's going to make this group happen."

'Then there was this guy called Jason, who was all full of himself because he'd been on *The Hit Man and Her*, and I was completely impressed. The fact that Jason had been on telly and liked RS2000 cars made him God in my eyes. He was cocky and strutty and I just thought he was great. Then, as I was halfway through my audition, in walks this other bloke called Howard – who was late, as always. And he was really shy. So that was the scenario. Take That met for the first time and I remember just looking round and thinking, Oh shit, I wish I'd passed my exams!

'Then Gary called me over and said, "Right, son – here's what you do." He called me "son"! He made me laugh from that moment on. He's got this brilliant northern humour and it's all really clever, quick one-liners. He's got loads of jokes – he is Gary "Bernard Manning/Roy Chubby Brown" Barlow. Me and him used to have some laughs.'

As the youngest member of the band and the last recruit, Robbie was very much junior to the others right from the start. He commuted to Manchester from Stoke-on-Trent (with Jan paying the £8 train fare), and input from him was neither expected nor wanted: the boys had a job to do and they were required to get on with it. Martin-Smith knew exactly what he wanted: a combination of disco, pop and soul, and he knew where to find it – in a producer called Ian Levine, who had formerly spent some time (unsuccessfully) trying to relaunch the careers of Tamla Motown stars.

'I learned working with those acts that you can't get a 17-year-old shop girl from Sheffield to go out and buy records by a 50-year-old soul group,' he said. 'She can't relate to it. But, if you take the same music, that clean-cut soul with high harmonies, give it a modern beat and lay it on a teenage boy group, it works.'

At first Robbie was not happy in his new life, and actually contemplated walking out before the band had even got off the ground. 'At that age, you think fame will be a joyous occasion, a fulfilled life and a Porsche 928,' he said, years after he finally did leave the band. 'But within a month I realised I hated the people I was with and they hated me. Then you feel trapped. You're too scared to leave and you don't want to stay. I walked out of rehearsal one day and went to see my dad. He was a bluecoat, working the holiday camps. I wanted to go on the road with him and leave the band, but he gave me a sobering lecture.

'He told me toilet rolls don't grow on trees, you have to buy them, you have to learn to do your laundry and iron, you have to buy food and cook for yourself. He made me realise what a tough life it could be when you don't earn much money, and then he said to me, "How are you going to feel when they are Number 1?" So I put my head down and stayed.

'The way the band was handled was things were divide and rule. The management wanted to elevate Gary Barlow and I was made to feel like a twat. Then you start believing them. I came out of the experience thinking I couldn't sing, that I had nothing to offer.'

While that last part is undoubtedly true, it may have been an exaggeration for Robbie to claim there was hate on all sides right from the start. The bitterness surrounding his actual departure was so great that it might have cast a shadow over everything, including the group's beginnings, but there were good times as well as bad. For a start, Robbie formed a friendship with Mark Owen and, secondly, he revelled in the spotlight when it eventually appeared. Without Take That, Robbie might never have hit the big time for, as the Spice Girls discovered a few years later, nothing can ever beat being in the right place at the right time.

His attitude might also have been overshadowed by the fact that it was very hard work. The band's choreographer, Kim Gavin, recalled Robbie's less than serious attitude to the job at hand. 'Rob didn't want to learn the routine, or he was the slowest,' he said. 'Everyone else would get up and go and have a break, and you'd have to go over it with him quite a few times. He'd make a joke of it, of course, but he was the last to learn.'

And it was hard slog. The newly formed band's first gig was in a nightclub in Huddersfield called Flicks and it was not an auspicious occasion. 'There were only about 20 people out there and a dog and only about 10 of those were interested in watching,' Gary commented later. They were paid the princely sum of £20, which, said Jason, 'paid for a Kentucky Fried Chicken for each of us'.

And so the sessions in gay clubs began, for which the boys were paid rather better – about £500 a time. 'At the beginning our following was totally gay,' Robbie said. 'Totally gay. At the start we did gay clubs and that – we all did. And it was fucking good groundwork for us. The gay clubs and the gay community – they embraced us with open arms.

'I think that anything the gay community comes up with will be dissed at first. Dismiss the music, dismiss the clothes, dismiss everything 'cos it's gay. And then, like, two to five years later, everyone's going, "Fucking hell! I'm mad for that music! I'm mad for those clothes!" And it's always the same: the gay community embraced us with open arms and then, before you know it, "Fucking hell, Take That, yeah. I've always quite liked them." Do you know what I mean? I suppose that was my first taste of fame. The first time I was totally approved of.'

New experiences were flowing in thick and fast. Asked about the greatest moment of his life in an interview after he'd left the band, Robbie confessed, 'I hate to admit it but it was when I took my first E. I don't want to advocate taking drugs – they mess you up, kids – but it was unbelievable. I was 17 and we were in this Spanish club – gay club, strangely enough – and the E was so strong. I was just, I love it here and I love you and I love me and I'm very funny and very handsome and very well endowed.' The E did, though, take its toll. On another occasion, Robbie said that he was at his happiest on E, but that it had a downside. His later depression, he said, was 'like the depression I used to feel after coming down from E. I wonder if it's because of drug abuse. Or maybe it's something to do with the weather.'

In keeping with their surroundings, the boys were going through a leather look – legend has it that the five of them were walking past Hyper Hyper on Kensington High Street in London when Jason saw a leather jacket with tassles, bought it and everyone else promptly purchased something else to match – while Martin-Smith began circulating demo tapes. He also managed to get the boys a spot on Sky TV, in which they performed two numbers and were subjected to a 10-minute interview. No one took the bait, so it was decided to release Take That's first single, 'Do What U Like', on the manager's own label, Dance UK. It was an act of faith on Martin-Smith's part – he had to remortgage his house to do it.

It scarcely made a ripple, charting at Number 82, but that was enough to spark interest in the industry and in September 1991, exactly a year after the band started, Take That signed a record contract with RCA. And the video that accompanied it more than bore witness to where the boys had been hanging out – it featured them writhing naked on the floor, smearing one another with jelly – and managed to get itself banned from primetime television.

When Take That first hit the big time, the boys were each given a £20,000 advance by the record company and Nigel Martin-Smith was adamant that this was only the beginning. Jeremy Marsh, who used to work at BMG, said, 'Nigel was clear from day one that this band were going to be, quote, global superstars, or at the very least huge at home.' He also had fond memories of the young star: 'Robbie was the youngest of the group and he was very much the cheeky chappy, the Norman Wisdom of the group.'

At that point, at least, the boys seemed to work happily together. 'We had a great time,' said Gary in an interview after Robbie left the band. 'We were all in

B&Bs. We'd get to our room and open the door and there'd be five single beds. I'd never had friends quite like these before. I hadn't been used to making sacrifices. I was quite a bold, selfish person at that time. And there was a bit of snobbery as well, because I was the musical one at the end of the day. But I grew to love these four people I was with. I can really understand why girls love Mark so much they can't go to sleep at night. I love Mark. He's one of the nicest people I know. I love Howard – he's probably my best friend in the band. I love Jason. And I loved Robbie when he was Robbie.'

It was not the end of Take That's fight to be famous – in fact, it wasn't even the beginning of the end. But it might have been the end of the beginning. The leather look was banished – teenage girls rather than gay men being the sought-after fan base – and, a month later, Take That's second single 'Promises' appeared. The boys were also showing themselves to be true professionals, appearing on everything from *Wogan*, *Pebble Mill* and *Going Live* to numerous live performances. The work seemed to pay off: 'Promises' entered the UK charts at Number 38. And then it all went wrong.

In retrospect, it was simply a case of the boys wanting the fame before the proper work had been done. They had built up a big gay following, but that was never going to make them into commercial giants and they had failed to build up grassroots support elsewhere. Their next single brought that home – entitled 'Once You've Tasted Love', it only made it to Number 44, despite the fact that the boys toured in conjunction with the Family Planning Association to promote awareness of safe sex. 'We're becoming the most famous group in Britain for not having a hit,' snapped Gary.

Others in the industry also began to wonder about the boys' future. 'We had been giving them a lot of space and, after their second single with RCA bombed, we wondered if we were flogging a dead horse,' said Mike Soutar, then editor of *Smash Hits* magazine, after they had finally made it. 'Other bands would have given up. They set out to find fame and fortune or whatever, find what they are looking for and don't like it. Take That are talented and resilient and have what it takes. The key to their success is that they are very hard working, are genuine good blokes and they are believable.'

In the longer run, the delayed entry to the big time probably did the group a favour. Their debut album was put on hold and the boys went all out to cultivate a fan base. It was a gruelling schedule, as the band performed four shows a day: a school gig during the day as part of the Big Schools Tour; an evening matinee; an under-18s club; and an over-18s club. They were singing for their supper as never before and it began to pay dividends.

'When we were first signed up by RCA, we did think we were going to make it straight away,' said Gary, after the group finally became famous. 'We didn't and we learned a lesson. We went round all the clubs, everywhere from schools, youth clubs, gay clubs – we covered the lot. We worked at the grassroots level because that's where it really counts. Fans don't just appear out of thin air. You have to make people like you, you have to give them something. By the time we released "It Only Takes A Minute", people from Doncaster to Devon and Dundee actually knew us from appearances right on their doorstep. Then, all of a sudden, it took off.'

But it was a miserable time in the interim. Radio 1 had refused to play 'Once You've Tasted Love', which had badly knocked its chances of success and demoralised the band, and the boys were reduced to living in a miserable bed and breakfast. No one was taking them seriously, with the more earnest (and pompous) sections of the music press calling them the 'pretty boys of pop'. They were beginning to think about giving up for good. Robbie, by now 17, was particularly depressed. 'It looks like we're just not going to make it,' he said despondently. 'It seems we're not going to have a hit record after all, and I'll just have to get a day job or go back to college. There's nothing left to do.' It was then that they learned that plans for their debut album had been put on hold. It was their lowest point.

It was Gary, the most musically experienced of the group, who was not prepared to go under. 'That was one of the most distressing times we ever had,' he recalled. 'We were building up a very loyal following with the fans, who came to see us wherever we played in the country. But still we couldn't convince some people we had what it takes. We were having some trouble getting our songs played on the radio and one or two DJs were downright nasty.

'I had been writing songs ever since I was 15, and even started playing cabaret in nightclubs when I was just 12. I knew in my heart that what I wanted to do was to make records and be in a band. It was when we heard that our third single was not going to be the hit we had prayed for that we all became so down in the mouth. But we fought back and I'm glad we did.'

The group's luck, according to none other than the *Daily Star*, finally changed when they staged a show at Hollywood's Disco in Romford, Essex. They had invited the pop editors of three newspapers, but the only people who showed up were the *Star*'s Rave team, who met the group for a drink and were then driven on to the gig in the band's 'That-mobile' – actually a minibus. They were particularly taken with Robbie, who entertained them with 'impressions of Norman Wisdom and Bros', before becoming even more impressed when they saw the show. Good old Rave then invited the band to play at a Christmas party in London's Limelight Club in front of 'dozens of VIPs' – and the band was, at long last, heading for the big time.

3
TAKE THAT –
AND PARTY

I 've had to change my telephone number a couple of times,' said Robbie. 'A few of the fans who work as operators found my number. Also a few fans' dads are policemen and they've been giving the girls my number. If I found out who it was, they'd be in serious trouble!'

The year was 1993, and Take That were at the height of their fame. There was no more touring school assembly halls, no more gay clubs and no more trying to convince the record industry that they had what it takes – the boys were on top of the world. The pressures might become too heavy to bear in time and, indeed, Robbie was to go spectacularly off the rails, but back then he was loving every minute of it. Still not yet 20, Robbie and the band had toured the world, notched up four hit singles (there were to be a further nine) and proved to the world that, yes, they really were back for good.

And back then, despite having to change his telephone number – as did the ever-present Nan, who also had to sell her house – Robbie was revelling in the attention brought by fame. In fact, looking back on that interview in *TV Hits*, the 19-year-old Robbie comes across as a picture of lost innocence. Here he is on football. 'I'm the best singer on the terraces! You should hear me harmonise. It's great because I live a stone's throw away from Port Vale football ground – I know it's a stone's throw away because I've broken all the windows! If girls are coming to the terraces and singing football songs with various swear words in them, then I suppose it is very romantic. I suppose when I get older I'll be romantic. I send flowers to people now and again. But the world is the limit when I'm in love. I would go anywhere, any time just to be with that certain person – it's just finding her! And I've never been anything but myself when chasing a girl!'

Not that Robbie and his cohorts had much time for chasing girls. 'To tell the truth,' he went on, 'we're working 100 per cent of the time and keeping so busy that we haven't had time to sit back and think that we've actually become a bit of a celeb-type thing. I mean, without sounding too blasé, it's a job. You could be a plumber fixing pipes or a carpenter or putting pipes down. I'm just singing in front of millions and millions of girls and being adored!'

There was just a hint of tension building up in the background when Robbie was asked if Gary had written most of the tracks for their next and second album, *Everything Changes*. 'Yeah, he's written all the stuff. He's loaded – I'm a pauper next to him! No, he wrote all the stuff, which we're happy about because it gives the band added credibility when you write your own stuff. I've actually just been listening to it and I'm so excited about the next album, more so than the last one, really.'

And, with hindsight, Robbie's description of the amount of time the band spent together makes interesting reading. 'I know it sounds sick but we do spend a lot of time together and we enjoy every minute of it. We live in each other's pockets 24 hours a day, seven days a week and we always manage to have a laugh. Even if we're having an argument, we always make a laugh out of the argument! It's a pleasure being with the guys ... they're a bunch of idiots, though. Except Mark!'

The reality, of course, was different. Robbie, the youngest and last recruit to the band, had always been something of a rebel, and Nigel Martin-Smith's very strict regime – no drink, no drugs, no steady girlfriends – was beginning to take its toll. Having been a keen drinker since he was 13, Robbie was now being offered all the other temptations available to a pop star and was taking advantage of them too – although hotly denying everything in public. Towards the end of 1992, he sparked a craze for sucking rubber dummies – after numerous public appearances in which he did just that

– until someone made the connection that ecstasy users suck dummies because it makes them want to chew.

'Please don't fret, I'm not on drugs,' said Robbie hastily. 'I have had lots of frantic letters from fans who are worried that I am hooked on drugs. I want to set their minds at rest. I don't take drugs and have no interest in them. We are a clean-living group. I know that dummies are connected with the ecstasy scene but that's not why I have them. The story behind my dummy couldn't be more innocent. A terrible spot came up just a few hours before I was due to do a photo shoot. I hit on the idea of sticking a dummy in my mouth to conceal it.'

It was an ingenious explanation, but one that was economical with the truth. A few years later, Robbie was to make that admission about taking ecstasy, adding that it was one of the best moment of his life. The real problem back then was not so much that Robbie was taking drugs, but that he had foolishly and inadvertently signalled his new habit to the rest of the world. For all his many and undoubted qualities, Robbie is not and never has been mature – and, by showing off, he revealed more than a member of a squeaky-clean boy band should.

The odd indiscretion aside, however, Robbie and Take That were having the time of their lives. In November 1992, with three Top 20 singles behind them – 'It Only Takes A Minute', 'I Found Heaven' and 'A Million Love Songs' – the boys embarked on their first tour as fully fledged pop stars rather than mere wannabes. They kicked off in Newcastle City Hall in front of a 2,000-strong audience, six of them men, with excited girls screaming at their new heartthrobs. The presence of those men, though, reminded everyone that the band's past had not been quite as squeaky clean as its present. 'We are happy to perform at gay clubs,' said Jason, when reminded of this. 'I'm really proud of our gay following. We get a lot of fan letters from men and I love reading them.' Robbie added, 'It's very flattering that both sexes fancy us.'

As far as girls were concerned, Robbie remained single, claiming at one point that he'd only managed to date three girls over the past year, 'But one of those times it was really good.' On another occasion he announced, 'There are three women in my life: my mum, Nan and sister.' This was exactly what the record company wanted to hear, of course: five single young men were a lot more attractive to the teen market than five young men with girlfriends. But, in Robbie's case, it was true. Never having been that much of a heartthrob at school, he was revelling in the life of a pop star, and especially the adulation of all those young girls.

And, behind the scenes, Robbie and the boys were doing what pop stars do. Just like their much wilder counterparts, the boys had groupies running after them with varying degrees of success. Robbie clearly remembered his first ever encounter with a hanger-on, which resembled nothing so much as a French farce.

'Take That hadn't been together long when we did a show on the Isle of Wight,' he recalled. 'Later we did an official meet and greet with some local girls. One was an absolute stunner. She was older than the rest, about 20, and, while we were all posing for a picture with the girls in front of us, she reached behind her and grabbed me in the most sensitive region. The photographer was snapping away and I was having the time of my life. I think I made him take about eight rolls of film.

'It suddenly struck me that she was a groupie – someone who liked sleeping with pop stars. Afterwards I told her to visit my hotel and gave her my room number. When we arrived back she was waiting for me outside the hotel. Nigel spotted her and ordered me back to bed. I went to my room and Mark came in to console me but suddenly there was a knock at the window. I peeped behind the curtains and the girl was standing there, topless. She hadn't spotted Mark, so I told him to hide in the wardrobe so he couldn't run off and tell Nigel.

'As I tried to pull her through the window, she screamed and woke Nigel in the room next door. He burst in to find this half-dressed lass stuck in the window, Mark laughing his head off inside the wardrobe and me still desperate to get my hands on my first groupie. He wasn't happy, to say the least. Mark was sent back to his room, the girl was sent packing and I had to have a cold shower.'

It was to be the first of many encounters with groupies, and the later trysts were very much more successful. 'Girls would always come back to our hotel after shows and we would often go down for drinks with them,' Robbie later recalled. 'If anyone took our eye, we'd chat them up and then try to get them into our room without Nigel or security finding out. I developed some truly extreme tactics. We were staying in Monte Carlo for the San Remo pop festival. We'd checked into the Loews hotel and some older girls had booked their own rooms, too. As we arrived one of them pushed her room number into my hand. I put it into my pocket before Nigel could see it and thought nothing more of it.

'After the show and a booze-up, I got back to my hotel room in the early hours. As I undressed, the scrap of paper with her number fell on the floor. In my drunken state, I managed to work out the girl's room was only seven or eight doors away. I couldn't risk the corridor in case our security guys spotted us, so I decided to climb over the balconies to get to her room.

'Unfortunately I was so sozzled that it wasn't until I was outside that I realised I was naked. I'd also forgotten that below was a long drop into the sea. But drink and the promise of a good-looking woman made me continue. I jumped over the balconies with surprising ease, amazingly found the right room and tapped on the window. The girl looked me up and down and, without flinching, opened the window and then pulled me through. I felt like the Milk Tray man – except that he never does his stunts naked.'

Even so, the act continued to bear echoes of the gay past. The boys would regularly strip on stage – although they never quite got everything off – frequently going down to their boxer shorts behind a see-through curtain. They would finish their numbers by turning their backs on the fans and whipping off their trousers to reveal the legend TA KE * TH AT on five pairs of underpants. It was a boy band, but one which appealed to boys – some boys, anyway – quite as much as it did to little girls.

The little girls, though, were blithely unaware of their heroes' other fan base – and were not averse to coming on strong to the band. They would camp outside the boys' hotels chanting, 'I want to see you naked', while the boys beamed, lapped it up and talked about the importance of safe sex. By January 1993, they had made a video for their next single, 'Why Can't I Wake Up With You', which was released in February – just as Robbie turned 19. The band won seven awards at the *Smash Hits* awards evening, which Robbie described as his career high to date. Plans were made to conquer the United States, with the five of them spending a fortnight in Manhattan – with Robbie fretting that he and Mark wouldn't be allowed into US clubs, which have a required age of entry of 21. The boys were still too young. 'I've always been excited about coming to New York but now that I'm here I don't know what I'll do if they won't let me go clubbing,' he fretted. 'I don't think I'll even be able to have a beer so I'm dead worried.'

Tour dates were set up abroad and Take That toured Japan and Europe. There was talk of movie deals – 'Robbie is hoping to meet Robert de Niro and Jason is already starting to think of himself as the new Keanu Reeves!' said Mark. Behind the scenes, however, Martin-Smith maintained rigid control, continuing to forbid the boys from having a private life – leading to rumours that they were all, in fact, gay.

'Flings and flirtations are fine,' he once said, 'but the real thing – sorry, no. Some people say it's not natural for guys of their age not to have regular girlfriends. I have never insisted that they behave like monks. But there's no room in their lives for heavy, serious relationships.'

Robbie was reportedly unconcerned. 'I have never had a steady girlfriend,' he said. 'The longest I have been out with anybody is three weeks. Long-term relationships are not me.' That failed to put the fans off – the group received 57,000 Valentine cards that year.

It was not only in the realm of relationships that Martin-Smith kept the boys on a tight leash. Shortly after winning a Brit award for Best Single with 'Could It Be Magic', on which Robbie sang lead vocals, it emerged that the band were living on the princely sum of £150 a week (with the possible exception of Gary, who had by now bought himself a £60,000 house). Nor did they seem to mind. 'We won't be making the same mistakes Bros did,' said Robbie brightly. 'Our £150 a week keeps us under control.' Not that there was much to pay for – they were fed and clothed by the record company, while Robbie, Mark and Howard were still living at home.

But, despite being known as the clown in the band, Robbie was beginning to show signs of a darker side to his personality. For a start, he confessed to believing in ghosts. Many people do, of course, but Robbie took this one step further. 'Sometimes I can't sleep because I can feel these spooky spirits,' he complained. 'A hotel we stay in is full of ghosts. I can't sleep there if I am on my own.' It seemed this had been going on since childhood. 'Once my dad came down and found me standing in the bar,' Robbie continued. 'He said, "What's up?" I told him I'd just seen a person we knew who'd died after being run over. He was waving at me, so my dad told me to wave back to him.'

It was not only ghosts that were beginning to bother him, but also the loss of a private life. For all the animosity that was to grow up between Robbie and the rest of the band in later years, at the time they played an enormous role in each other's lives. 'The lads are like my family – the people I want to love and who give me love,' said Robbie, open as ever. 'When I am not with my own family, the band take their place. I would have to kill myself if any of the lads died.' But the pressures of fame were showing. 'I used to enjoy going out with the lads, going to a club, getting drunk, falling over, having a laugh – even doing runners from taxis,' he lamented. 'But I can't do that any more. I can't go out to the pub and be a normal lad because there are people who want to watch me drinking.'

Teen excitement built as the UK leg of the tour resumed and, by July 1993, when the band played Manchester, home city to all of them except Robbie, it had reached hysteria level. The band were trapped inside a police van by their frenzied admirers when they turned up for a photo session with Manchester United. Minders had to form a human corridor for the boys to be able to make their way into Old Trafford.

With their single 'Pray' at its second week at Number 1, the crowd was 9,000-strong, when the boys played Manchester's G-Mex Centre, with many of the children playing truant from school beforehand in order to catch a glimpse of the fab five. 'Take the roof off!' cried Robbie as the concert began: the fans obliged and the boys gained even more popularity when they donated the proceeds of the concert to United skipper Bryan Robson's £1.5 million appeal to buy cancer-detecting equipment for Royal Manchester Children's Hospital. The boys were proving themselves to be generous all round, especially Robbie – it emerged that, when he got his first pay packet, he promptly paid Nan's gas bill.

The circus carried on to Wembley, accompanied by the usual stories about teen spending sprees in the group ('My mum is really angry that I've spent £100'), which one kissed best (Mark – Robbie stuck to the fans' cheeks), which one was most fanciable (Mark), which one was most sensitive (Howard) and which one was making the most money (no prizes for guessing, Gary). And it was after the Wembley concert that Robbie first met a woman who was to play a part in his adult life – Kylie Minogue.

'She's gorgeous and frail,' said an awestruck Robbie. 'You feel like you want to protect her and keep her under your wing. Unfortunately, none of us are allowed girlfriends at the moment, so we can only remain the best of friends.' The concert itself was deemed a triumph and the boys were whisked off to an after-show party, followed by a short break – and then it was back to the recording studios, again.

The game plan was working. In December 1993, the boys swept the boards for the second time at the *Smash Hits* readers' poll and it was not just for their music: as well as Best Group, Best Album and Best Pop Video, Mark was pronounced Most Fanciable Male Star and Best Dressed Person; Jason got Best Dancer in Pop; and a newly shorn Robbie walked off with Best Haircut.

It seemed the boys could do no wrong. One particularly inexplicable phenomena at the time was Mr Blobby, a man hiding inside a huge rubber suit covered with blobs that originated in Noel Edmonds's *Noel's House Party*. The creature had got to Number 1 with something called 'The Blobby Song'. Take That easily knocked him off his perch with 'Babe', their third Number 1, for Christmas 1993 – and for that alone they should be remembered with pride. 'We dedicate it to all our fans who have been with us since the beginning,' said a delighted Robbie.

It was at this time that rumours began to circulate that someone wanted to leave the band – Gary. He had always been seen as the creative genius behind the five of them and, as the songwriter behind 'Babe', he clearly began to feel he deserved a career on his own, not least as the likes of Sir Elton John, later to be a saviour to Robbie, were expressing an interest. 'Elton John has said he would love to work with him, which is a great compliment, and Gary is flattered, but I can't say any more,' said an RCA spokesman. Gary himself began to talk about leaving England for Los Angeles. 'That's where the music industry is,' he said, 'and where I will be free to live my life how I want.'

Much to the fans' relief he stayed – at which point Robbie became the focus of attention. He had, after all, initially wanted to be an actor, and in April 1994 there was a real possibility that he would leave the group to carve out a new career in the movies. Now 20, he had been offered a £1 million role in an American film but, with their latest single 'Everything Changes' at Number 1, and in the middle of a sell-out European tour, he decided to stay put.

'I have been screen-tested for several roles and was offered a big part in a major American movie,' he said. 'But I turned it down because I just couldn't fit it all in. I am very interested in acting but, once I found out how much work was involved and the amount of time it would end up taking, I knew I just would not be able to do it. It would have meant several months' work away from the guys in the group. And I wouldn't have been able to tour with Take That this summer.

'I hope it will be an option in the future because it has always been something I wanted to do. When I was younger, I even thought I would end up as an actor rather than a pop singer. Maybe, in a few years' time, there might be a break in Take That's schedule that will allow me to do some acting.'

Certainly, there seemed to be no reason to leave just then. The boys actually made musical history that year, when 'Everything Changes', the single from the album of the same name, became their fourth single to go straight into the charts at Number 1, a feat unmatched by the likes of The Beatles and Elvis. The other three singles – 'Pray', 'Relight My Fire' and 'Babe' – had also come from the same album. Robbie, like the rest of the boys, was delighted. 'We are just over the moon. We've been jumping around our rooms pinching ourselves just to check it's true,' he said from Munich, where the band was on tour.

With all this adulation, it was almost inevitable that Take That would be awarded the next accolade for any group worth its salt – a tribute band. Called Fake That, it was initially a gimmick dreamed up by Channel 4's *The Big Breakfast*, which appealed for 'ringers for the singers' to take part. First to be signed up was one David Brice, a 23-year-old builder from Liverpool who bore a strong resemblance to Robbie, and promptly started being courted by record companies keen on a deal. Such was Take That's popularity at the time that even fame by association turned to gold.

David was thrilled. 'When the competition for Fake That was launched, there were no plans to release a song,' he said. 'But I have been approached by a record company, which wants to sign up the rest of the winners. At first when people stopped me in the street, I thought it was a bit of a giggle. It became even better when bouncers would call me up to the front of the queue at a club. But I never thought it would lead to a record deal and getting my face on telly.'

The other four were quickly chosen and promptly began to attract almost as much attention as the originals, bringing traffic to a halt, having fans swooning and screaming and standing in at clubs when they couldn't get the real thing. David, for one, was thoroughly enjoying himself. 'I've had my first taste of fame and I love it,' he said. 'Give me the bright lights, the girls and the bubbly any time. Now I've been in Robbie's shoes for a while, I find it a comfy fit.' Nor were they the only ones. One group of girls adopted the band's Christian names and said they wanted to do cover versions of the boys' hits under the name of Take This, while two more outfits styled themselves Take Me and This And That. Everyone, it seemed, wanted a piece of the action.

Not that the boys themselves were unduly perturbed,

for not only is imitation the sincerest form of flattery, but they were living it up in Australia at the time. And they were going down a storm. The 17-date tour had introduced them to a whole new set of fans, with 'Pray' entering the Top 5, and a sell-out concert at the Wonderland theme park in Sydney. Each band member seemed to be enjoying himself: Howard had even written a song himself, 'If This Is Love', which was included on the *Everything Changes* album. He in particular was over the moon. 'I want this life to last forever,' he said. 'I don't think I could cope without it' – although, when the time came, of course, he did.

And their schedule in Australia was quite as gruelling as it was back home. The boys were working 14-hour days, appearing not only in concert but at interviews and television performances as well. But they remained cheerful, splashing around in the sea and attempting handstands and backflips, and joshing with one another, as friends do. Mark was dubbed 'Clint' after he took to wearing a cowboy hat, while Robbie was named 'The Perv' after sporting a hat with the slogan 'Pervert' on it, handed to him by a fan. Jason, meanwhile, was called 'Beadle' because of his habit of taking pictures of anything and everything. 'It's cool to be here!' said Robbie. 'I've topped up my tan and met loads of great people!' And then, with barely a second to spare, it was back to Britain and a 36-date tour in August.

And so to what was possibly their most successful night so far: the 1994 *Smash Hits* Poll Winners' Party in

December. The boys won every prize they were up for, including Best Group in the World, Best British Group and Best Haircut (Robbie again) – and then made it into the *Guinness Book of Records* courtesy of the 12,500 screaming fans present that night. The noise they made registered 115.3 decibels, the loudest ever recorded at a concert. 'If you put your ear next to a pneumatic drill it would reach about 100, so it was pretty loud,' said a spokesman for the *Guinness Book of Records*. Take That hardly paused: they rushed to Berlin where they won the even more prestigious MTV award as the World's Best Group.

In fact, Take That were at the absolute height of their fame and success and, for a band designed to appeal to young teenagers, it would have been almost impossible to stay at those heights forever. The only ones who ever managed it went on to appeal to older audiences and that is something the boys, with varying degrees of success, went on to do individually, not as a band. And the strains of life at the top were more in evidence than ever. Despite all the protestations about being one another's best friends, the boys were beginning to find it impossible to lead anything like a normal lifestyle. The older ones, in particular, were beginning to complain about not being allowed a proper girlfriend, while the younger ones simply wanted to have fun.

And, on top of everything else, the boys were exhausted. They had been working hard for four years now, three of those as international superstars, and they badly needed a rest. In fact, according to Jason, at one stage they nearly missed a concert because they were just too tired to go on. 'We were all backstage at Wembley Arena and we were all tired because we'd done so many gigs,' he said. 'We didn't really want to go on stage because we were so tired. Then we heard the news that we were Number 1 in the charts with "Sure" and that perked us up. It was the best present ever.'

But it was also a sign of things to come. Well aware that most bands have only a limited shelf life, everyone involved was keen to get the boys to do as much as they could while they were still on top – and it was taking its toll. By this time the boys could barely go to the loo without an attendant bodyguard to ward off the fans, and even bigger and better plans were afoot for 1995, when there was to be another attempt to take on America. Jason, one of the older members of the band, could see the pitfalls. In private, he declared, Robbie could 'go off the rails' simply to make up for missing out on so much of his teenage years.

Not that the others were feeling much better. 'We'll get a bit of time off at Christmas,' Jason continued. 'I want to go home to see me mum and change me underwear – only joking! But we do start to chill out over Christmas a little bit. That's what we're trying to do, anyway.'

And it wasn't just the band that was suffering – it was their nearest and dearest as well, particularly Robbie's mother, Jan. Completely fed up with living under siege from hysterical Take That fans, Christmas 1994 proved the final straw. More than 40 teenagers set up camp around Jan's 1930s three-bedroom semi on Greenbank Road, Tunstall, which Robbie still used as his home when he was not on tour, leading Jan to send out a note asking for privacy. The fans, from all over Europe as well as Britain, ignored her request which finally led to Robbie, friendly, gregarious, joker Robbie, appearing in person and telling them to 'go away'. They refused.

'I've travelled 900km and waited four hours just to be snubbed,' complained Natalie Gansauge, 20, from Dortmund.

Other fans couldn't understand that there might be a problem, even though they were actually painting messages to Robbie on nearby properties. 'I forgive him for being arrogant,' said 16-year-old Rebecca Barton from Chelmsley, Birmingham. 'To see his bum was worth waiting for.'

Jan had had enough. She put the house on the market for £57,950 – prompting enquiries to local estate agents not from potential buyers but from people who really wanted to look at Robbie's 7ft 9in by 7ft 8in bedroom. 'The family have enjoyed living here for several years,' said a sympathetic neighbour, 'but they're fed up with it. This is the price Robbie has had to pay for his superstar status.'

Robbie was to pay a good deal more before it was all over – if, indeed, it ever will be – but something was bound to break. Robbie was very talented, but kept on a leash so tight that it was about to snap. Nor could he even have a quiet night in with his mother without coming under siege. And, as Jason had so presciently remarked, Robbie had missed out on most of his teens: just 15 when he signed up with the group, he had never been able to live out a normal adolescence – and that after a childhood haunted by the absence of his father.

Much has been made in later years about Robbie's slightly odd attitude to sex – he seems to find it easier to sleep with groupies than girlfriends, and that's even before questions about his sexuality are taken into account – which almost certainly stems from his time with Take That. Although he lost his virginity while still at school, his first real experience of adult sexuality was in the gay bars that the boys started out in. Whether or not Robbie ever had a homosexual experience himself, and he has always denied it, that time must have made some impact on him. The vast majority of teenagers go through a phase during which they are attracted to the same sex, and in all likelihood Robbie was going through exactly that at the time that he was surrounded by gay men. It's hardly a surprise that he's joked about the subject, and the truth about his own sexuality, ever since.

And then there were the girls. Behind the clean-living image, there had been drink, drugs and girls – this was, after all, the world of rock 'n' roll. Some years later, Robbie admitted that he took full advantage of the girls on offer – and there were a lot of them – 'Of course I snogged fans,' he said several years after leaving the group. 'I was 18, 19, 20 and my hormones were raging. There were always hundreds of them staying in the hotels. I used to nick Gary Barlow's as well.'

All told, it's a wonder they stayed together as long as they did. Take That took to the road in 1995, with no idea that they were nearing the end – and it was Gary, no less, who gave a very affectionate interview about the boys. 'I know how much we love doing what we do,' he said. 'At the moment, I could not imagine my life without Take That. I would miss all the laughs, all the friendship and all the people we know. I really miss everyone when we have time off. The best vibe for me is swapping stories. We are the best of mates and anyone who knows us will vouch for that.'

Mark added something along the same lines. 'I can imagine that we will be around in 20 years' time,' he said. 'Of course, we would be doing something totally different. But I see us all being together and being good mates.'

The interview came out in July, after months of rowing, claim and counterclaim. But back then, at the beginning of 1995, no one, Robbie included, had a clue as to what lay ahead.

Robbie did have one thing on his mind, though. After years of living in the cocooned state of Take That Towers, as he called it, he came to a decision – one that was to change the face of British pop. He decided to go to Glastonbury.

4

ROBBIE WILLIAMS, NUTTER

The world of showbusiness – and of teenyboppers – was stunned. Robbie Williams had broken free of Nigel Martin-Smith's reins in quite spectacular style. He had turned up at Glastonbury, one of Europe's largest and wildest music festivals, with bleached blond hair, a blacked-out front tooth and a couple of gallons of champagne. He was pictured drinking this champagne while waving a cigarette around and, worse still, he was hanging out with the bad boys of rock, Noel and Liam Gallagher. He was signing autographs 'Robbie Williams, nutter'. Everyone was utterly bemused, with the exception of four young men and their manager. They were quite simply appalled.

Robbie Williams simply could not go along with the charade any longer. He was just 21 and had spent the last six years (well, the last four anyway) pretending to be super squeaky clean. In reality, he wasn't – very few young men are at that age. But, whereas the other members of Take That were prepared to keep their private behavior private, Robbie, the youngest of the group and the one who had missed out on having a normal teenage lifestyle most, simply could not bear it any more.

It was actually the second time Robbie had been to Glastonbury, but the first, a year previously, had been spent hiding from photographers inside M People's tour bus. This time, he was going to do it properly. 'I nicked 16 bottles of champagne, put them in the boot of this blacked-out Jag and drove to Glastonbury. Drunk a bottle of champagne on the way.'

There was not much chance of anyone missing him. Robbie was pictured with the boys from Pulp, played football with the Boo Radleys and cavorted with Simon from Menswear. And while he says he can't remember a good deal of it now, he knew exactly what he was doing. 'Unauthorised TV interviews and photos were forbidden by our management,' he said. 'So at Glastonbury I thought, I'm going to do exactly what I want. I made sure I got my picture taken, and I did every TV show in the place. I'd had enough.'

And finally, as the *pièce de résistance*, Robbie appeared on stage with Oasis. 'Liam just went, "Come on," and that was it, really. It's interesting though, isn't it? That there was a moment when it [the conversion from pop to rock] actually crystallised.' In fact, the conversion was so complete that Robbie dumped the Jag and made his way back in a roadie's van.

That was not all. Robbie was beginning to want to be taken seriously as a musician and at Glastonbury he was mixing with the people he wanted to be – especially the Gallaghers. 'I was a bit apprehensive at first,' he admitted in an interview some months later, 'because you read all this stuff about Noel and Liam and the lads, and I was wondering how they were going to take me. But it was top. I walked in and Liam goes, "Take fucking what?" And that was it. I knew we'd have a laugh.'

There had been signs for some time that all was not well in Take That Towers. 'It was obvious that, when we went on promotional trips, I'd just take myself off to a club or to dinner or to whatever,' said Robbie. 'Not that I was disliking anybody's company, I just wanted to be myself. And when I went off to Glastonbury, I think that was the straw that broke the camel's back.'

And matters quickly went from bad to worse. Not content with living it up with the bad boys of Oasis, Robbie went on MTV's *Most Wanted* show and dropped his trousers for a bet. 'That's the most satisfying £10 I have ever earned,' he said. He turned up at an awards ceremony with his hair cut into Johnny Rotten-style blonde spikes. He gave interviews that most emphatically did not toe the line. 'I'm 21. I'm in Britain's biggest band but I'm bored out of my brains,' he said. 'I'm not really like the rest of the band. I like going mad, I like having a great time and I don't like being told what to do. At Glastonbury, people looked at me like I was a zit at the end of their nose because I'm a member of Take That. They think I'm a total prat.'

They weren't the only ones. The rest of Take That and Nigel Martin-Smith were beside themselves. What might have been contained as a bit of youthful high spirits was turning into a PR disaster for the band, not least because Robbie would not shut up. He had bottled it all up for years, it seemed, and now it was all tumbling out.

'There can be times when I feel I'm still at school,' he said. 'I was 17 [sic] when I got involved in the band and I never really got the chance to do what other teenagers do. When you're in a band like this, it can be like being in the army. You have to get up at a certain time, go out at a certain time, eat certain things and every single second of your day is accounted for. When we're on tour we have to ring each other up to say what we're going to be wearing that night just in case we end up wearing the same thing.'

He wanted to try acting, he said. He had been forced to turn down the role of Robin in *Batman and Robin* because of touring commitments, he said. He wanted a break he said. 'I do love all the guys and I know I've been really lucky to be part of such an amazing thing,' he said.

But attempts to patch things up were disastrous. When Robbie was finally reunited with his old teammates, they were unable to disguise their disgust. 'I came back and I was like, "Hi, boys! Glastonbury was top! You're not gonna believe it! I was with Jarvis of Pulp, I was with Oasis, they're top!"' he recalled. 'I was like – and some fell on stony ground. Do you know what I mean? They were like "Really? Oh. Let's rehearse." So they had a meeting about my behaviour. Again.'

For a time no one seemed to know what was happening. Robbie disappeared again, amid confusion about whether or not he was still actually in Take That. 'We don't know where Robbie is,' said Gary. 'We just want him to get in touch with us so we can tell him everything's okay.'

Mark was less discreet. 'We had an agreement as a band to give six months' notice if anyone wanted to leave or fancied doing something different,' he said in an interview on Radio 1, in July 1995. 'He broke the news to us about two weeks ago. He gave us his six months' notice, really. Since then we have been trying to carry on in rehearsal, but it was obvious he wasn't happy. So we decided maybe as a mate we didn't want to put him through this pain for six months and maybe he should go now.'

The reality was slightly different. Robbie had been sacked by an incandescent management – and one that had, after all, originally planned on a four-person band. But it seemed that someone somewhere had forgotten that Take That had found success with five of them – and that Robbie was one of the most popular members of Take That. Robbie himself, although he'd known he was courting trouble, was stunned when he found out that this was the end.

'I was looking at all these faces and it was just like a whirl of, "What the fuck do I do in this situation? This was never in my game plan!"' Robbie said. 'And macho bravado came across to cover up. I was like, "Oh, you want me to go then? Well, can I take that melon?"' Clutching the melon, Robbie went outside and climbed into a car with his driver and security man to be driven home to Stoke-on-Trent. 'It was the weirdest journey that I've ever been on,' said Robbie, 'with these two people not knowing what to say or do and me not knowing whether to laugh, cry, throw myself out of the window – or phone up a few bands to see if they needed a vocalist. And that was it. The end of an era for me. And you know what? I don't even like melon.'

There are conflicting accounts about who made the final decision that Robbie had to go, but it was by no means unanimous – Mark burst into tears upon being told that Robbie was leaving the band. And if everyone had thought they could carry on as before, they soon found themselves very much mistaken. Teenagers the world over were distraught, with attention focused on, of all places, Berlin, where the band had performed that spring.

Hotlines were set up for Robbie fans who wanted to share their pain, and many did – the hotline received hundreds of calls. One poor little girl tried to kill herself, and another 50 held a vigil outside Berlin's Hilton hotel, home to the boys during the tour. Grouped under a banner reading 'Robbie Come Back, We Need You', the girls set about collecting a petition to send to MTV. 'How can we accept the fact that Robbie's leaving?' asked Carola Berger, 20. 'He's got to reconsider, he doesn't know what he's doing to us,' sobbed Petra, 13. 'The group's management is to blame,' said Ineke Kleinschmidt, 14. 'I can't believe he'd go voluntarily.'

Robbie's departure even made the *News At Ten*. The staff at *Boyz*, a gay magazine, wore black armbands for a week.

The remaining boys tried to put a brave face on it. 'When Robbie first announced he wanted to leave, of course we were all devastated,' said Mark, who clearly was. 'We did even think about splitting up. But we love what we do so much and have so much to look forward to, with the new single and tour, that we feel we couldn't possibly call it a day.'

Gary also chipped in. 'The four of us are still 100 per cent committed to this band and are very much looking forward to a long future together,' he said. The fans were not so sure, shouting out Robbie's name when the newly depleted Take That appeared on *Top Of The Pops*.

As for Robbie himself – he was in a state of shock. Anxious to avoid the world's press when he was still so unsure as to where his future really lay, he headed to just about the most unlikely location possible – Carmarthen Bay holiday camp in Kidwelly, near Swansea. The camp is owned by Andrew Brown, a friend of Robbie's father, and provided sanctuary at a very difficult time. 'Robbie stayed with us when he said he was leaving the band,' Brown said after Robbie left. 'He was going through a tough time. His future lies in pop and he wants to carry on singing. But at the moment he wants to be left alone.'

And, amongst all the trauma of finding himself newly alone, Robbie was beginning to appreciate the advantages of leaving the band. 'Quitting was no mistake,' he said to fans at the two-day pop festival T In The Park in Lanarkshire. Sporting a new, brown hairstyle, he continued, 'And, even if my new solo career doesn't take off, I really won't be sorry that I left. Now I've quit, I must admit it's good to be able to go to the toilet without a minder at my side. I can remember when people used to treat me normally. People keep saying I must be really sad and miserable now, but that's not really it. I miss the normal way I used to be able to walk down the street.'

He had been warned of the perils of über-celebrity – and it was by someone who knew what he was talking about. 'I met Jordan Knight from New Kids On The Block once and asked him how he handled it all when they were on top,' said Robbie. 'He said to me, "Just don't let anyone wipe your backside." At the time I thought it was mad, but now I understand exactly what he meant. The more decisions that are made for you, the more backward you become. The decisions I'm making now might be wrong, but at least they're mine.'

In fact, Robbie was beginning to seethe underneath. In public the myth was being maintained that it was he who had decided to walk out, but Robbie – and the boys and Nigel Martin-Smith – knew that in reality he had been given no choice. And it was a tough way to treat him. Robbie had been in the band since he was little more than a child, had been expected to comply with a fairly harsh regime and had now been turfed out at the first sign of trouble, with little support from anyone.

And he was beginning to assess the last few years. 'The restrictions were phenomenal,' he said. 'Now I think, You dick, why did you stay in the band for so long? Well, I had no other option. I joined because I left school with no qualifications and was scared about what my mum would say. I auditioned for this band just to keep out of trouble.' Why, he was asked, had he not left before? 'When you've been conditioned from an early age, it stays with you. I'm still not free from the shackles of "Can I do this, can I do that?" When you take the shackles off someone's wrists, their wrists are still bruised.' Are the bruises getting better? 'Yeah,' said Robbie. 'I've got some ointment.'

And he was learning about real life again. 'When I came home after being on the road with Take That, I would be totally lost,' he said. 'My mum would say, "Rob, what do you want for dinner?" and I'd be bemused. I never had to make decisions like that. On the road I had people fannying around after me the whole time.'

Robbie was also beginning to realise that, in leaving a band that was, to put it bluntly, cheesy, he had finally turned into the kind of cool pop star he had always wanted to be. 'I've had an excellent reaction from the British public,' he enthused. 'I think they wanted one of Take That to show that they cared about reality. In Take That we had to tell so many lies, it feels good to be myself at last. I'm suddenly signing boys' names on autographs as well as girls'. It's a real ego thing for me because I've always wanted to be respected by my peers. That never really happened in Take That.'

Another survivor of a boy band, George Michael, was a help. 'He didn't give me any advice about it, it was just the weekend I left or got sacked from the band, I went away and he was there,' said Robbie. 'We just chatted and, of course, if anybody's going to know what the dealings with record companies are like or leaving bands, it's gonna be him. So whatever advice he gave would have been good. We were talking about music, football and fruit.'

If Robbie thought that breaking free from his old friends was going to be easy, though, he had another think coming. For a start, he simply did not know what to do. Every move he had made for the last six years had been on the orders of someone else: now there was no one. And there was also the small matter of a looming lawsuit with his record company, from which Robbie eventually withdrew. He had been suing RCA for the freedom to be allowed to record elsewhere, but in the end the matter was settled out of court, with Robbie agreeing to abandon the action and pay RCA's legal costs in early 1996. So, back in the beginning, he appeared for a week on *The Big Breakfast* and then set off the way he meant to continue. He partied.

The following months were a blur. Robbie hung out at Browns nightclub in London with Oasis, and partied in St Tropez with George Michael, Bono, Paula Yates and Michael Hutchence. No celebrity event was complete without Robbie and, free of the constraints that had bound him for so long, he took full advantage of it.

Only once in his heroic endeavour to attend every celebration in the free world did he encounter his old friends: at the Brit Awards in February 1996. It was not an auspicious occasion. Mark waved and said, 'Look after yourself.' The others seemed to ignore him. Robbie's bitterness intensified.

That Brit Awards, though, marked yet another momentous occasion in the life of Take That: namely, the split. Whether or not the band's break-up had come about because of Robbie's departure seven months earlier – and, to be fair to the remaining foursome, they did make it to Number 1 in the album charts with *Nobody Else* and Number 1 in the singles with 'Never Forget' without him – the boys realised they had reached their sell-by date. As far back as 1995, Gary had mused at the end of the tour, 'I stared out into the crowd, and realised that the flat-chested 13-year-old girls who had helped make us stars were now 18-year-olds with boobs.'

A last single, a cover version of the Bee Gees' 'How Deep Is Your Love' ('It should be called "How Deep Are Your Pockets",' snapped Robbie), was to appear at the end of February and then that was it. The boys left the stage with a good deal of grace. 'We've decided we have done all we can as Take That,' said Mark. 'We took it to a level well beyond any of our expectations and, I suppose, beyond many of your expectations.'

Jason chipped in. 'There have been so many sob stories from has-been pop stars complaining about loss of money, fast cars and fast women,' he said. 'But we would like to say today that we have had an absolutely brilliant time. It's been absolutely wicked.'

The usual hysteria ensued, with one newspaper commenting that the news 'prompted an immediate outbreak of largely pre-pubescent trauma. And that was only among the pop press.' ChildLine hastily set up a hotline for grief-stricken tweenies; the band promised to do the same. One final concert date was set for Holland in April and that was it. With seven Number 1 hits, four million single sales and three million album sales behind them, the boys were about to take their final bow.

Robbie was quite restrained given the circumstances. 'Frankly, I am more concerned about how Port Vale do in the cup tonight, but Take That were six years of my life and I know how the guys are feeling,' he said.

He was also able to paint an accurate description of what caused the band to split up. 'Take That was a time bomb that was inevitably going to go off,' he said. 'It's like if you're a kid and you get a pair of shorts, you can't be expected to wear that same pair of shorts for the next 15 years.'

He was quite right, but he was dealing with problems of his own, problems that were threatening to get out of hand. For a start, he was beginning to hit the bottle, big time, as he acknowledged later in that same year. 'After being locked away for so long, I had to get out, but now I wish I hadn't gone out so much,' he said. 'It wasn't an answer to my problems – it added to them because I'd just wake up the next day with my problems and a hangover. I got drunk and fell over a lot, I wasn't happy. And I never had a drink problem, no matter what the papers said. Not having anything to do was the hardest thing. I let myself waste away doing nothing, and for a while I bought into that rock 'n' roll thing. I jumped from one myth to another. It was a security blanket.'

Gary, perhaps surprisingly, was still showing a great deal of magnanimity towards his old chum. 'I can't believe some of the things Robbie's said. He's spoken so much rubbish,' he said. 'Robbie was my friend for five years. I really loved him and I want him to make a hit record. Robbie was the best performer in Take That. If people were to see him on stage, he would blow them away. I want to hear him sing and give me goosepimples like he used to.

'No matter what he has done, Robbie's talent will outshine all of it. We invested a lot in Rob. When he joined the group he was overweight and he couldn't learn the dance routines, but we stood by him, we helped him and we've been nothing but faithful. But I'm still here and when he turns back into the Rob I knew and loved I'll be here again. If he ever hits rock bottom or if he ever wants anything, then I would give it to him and I hold my hand on my heart when I say that. He's a bit of a time bomb at the moment and the last thing he needs is me ringing him up. When the time's right, we'll meet again. Definitely.'

Robbie was not so generous in return. He wanted to get back to work but was hampered by an ongoing lawsuit. Nor did he feel the need to be nice about his exes, calling Gary a 'clueless wanker' and the rest of them as 'selfish, arrogant and thick'. For some reason, he then changed his mind and apologised. 'I want to phone Gary and tell him how sorry I am,' he announced to *Smash Hits*. 'What must he think of me? The stupid thing is I didn't mean it. Those aren't my feelings. Gary's kept himself together, even though I've tried very hard to rattle his cage. I thought he was going to call me a shit and he hasn't, so fair play.'

Gary, on the verge of his own solo career, could not resist a reply. 'I'm disappointed in Robbie,' said Gary in an interview with *Media Arena Magazine* in May 1996. 'He's taken a different road from us. I can't say it's wrong because I don't know where he's at really, but

I'm just very disappointed in the way he's turned out. A lot of the things he's said in articles have hurt us all – he was a prisoner in Take That, that none of us are close friends, that we've never been friends. It's complete rubbish. We're all so close and we've always been close.

'He'd always been Mark's best friend. Jason and Howard were a bit of a clan and Mark and Robbie were another. I would never join Mark and Robbie, I'd always join Jason and Howard because they were that little bit older. Mark grew up and became a very truthful, good-living person. He got into Buddhism – he became a very interesting person, I thought. And I think he left Robbie behind and Robbie resented that.

'We were doing dance routines on stage and Robbie was doing his own routine. We were afraid to say, "Robbie, you dickhead, fucking get it together. We're a five-piece band here." We couldn't do that any more: he was a bit of a loose cannon. He'd missed out on his teenage years and he wanted to live them now.' Gary continued that Robbie was developing 'a following of really funny people, not the sort of people we'd ever been friends with – real trendies'.

'Every other week he'd be in the paper coming out of a club with a girl on his arm. And it wasn't our image, that. There wasn't a rulebook, but we'd always been aware of the guidelines, of what we could and couldn't do. Because part of the charm of Take That was that nobody could ever get near them: nobody was an insider, there was no scandal, there were no wild parties.

When we arrived it was beautiful: nice wave, we'd do the gig and we were home. But all of a sudden, people had an in, and it was Robbie.

'We thought, We'd like to do that. We'd like to go in and out of clubs and get drunk and have girls and not worry about being seen. We said to Robbie, "Cool it, Rob. Be a bit more shady about it." But Robbie was on a complete rebellion at this point. I don't think he ever liked the music in Take That very much and he certainly didn't like the tours because they were so energetic. That meant he couldn't be up until six in the morning: he had to get some sort of rest to be able to get through the show. It was all coming to a head about the time of Glastonbury in June last year, when we heard he'd been on the stage with Oasis. That felt shocking at the time.'

In fact, Robbie and Gary were about to go head to head. Both had new records out: Robbie with a cover version of George Michael's song 'Freedom' (the symbolism of that was lost on nobody) on his new record label Chrysalis – he was believed to have signed a £2 million deal – and Gary with 'Forever Love'. Gary got in first and got to Number 1, Robbie followed with 'Freedom' and only made it to Number 2. Ten love to Gary.

'I don't think Robbie quite knows where he wants to go,' said one industry insider. 'What he has in his favour is a great personality. His challenge is going to be to have the confidence to develop his own musical identity. There is a lot of money riding on him now and he has to watch that he doesn't get submerged by this corporate machine. I think there will be a clash at some point.'

Robbie himself was a good deal more nervous than he let on at the time. 'At the press conference to launch my solo career I was terrified – no one could tell, but when I got on that stage I was dead nervous,' he confessed later. 'My hand was shaking so much I didn't dare pick up my glass of water! The people you think are most confident are probably the most shy as well.'

I didn't help that it took Robbie some time to find the right people to manage him. His first manager post-Take That was Kevin Kinsella, who ran Jelly Street Management. Robbie had fled to Kevin and his wife Norma soon after leaving the band and stayed with them in their house in Cheshire. It was not an easy time.

'There were problems from the moment I took him on,' Kevin said. 'We met him off the plane, me and his mum, when he came back from George Michael's place in the south of France where he went after he had been sacked. I got him home to my house and he just broke down crying. He was in a terrible state. He was living with us for three months while the whole country's press was trying to find him. He was on drugs and booze, and was messed up. At the time, he was probably on a bottle of vodka and a bottle of Bacardi a day. He was picking up these bottles and saying, "Can you get me more?"'

The association didn't last long – Robbie stayed with

Kevin for just six months, during which time he did that stint on *The Big Breakfast*. But Kevin was never in any doubt that one day his protégé would pull himself together and regain his star status. 'There was no single turning point when he pulled himself together,' he said. 'Rob always believed he was going to be a star. Whatever anyone else said, he was going to be a star and I believed him. He had that aura, that presence, without a doubt.'

However, despite the launch of his new career, the war of words with his exes continued. Robbie continued to lash out in an attempt to come to terms with the past few years. 'I hate to shatter the myth, but Take That as you know them don't exist,' he said. 'I know it's a crap comparison, but Take That and the Loch Ness monster aren't too dissimilar because Take That live beneath the surface and never show who they really are. You've got more chance of seeing the real Loch Ness monster than the real Take That.'

Battle intensified. 'If I sat next to Gary on a plane I would feel uncomfortable,' said Robbie, before going on to call Gary 'clueless, dated, selfish, stupid and greedy'.

Gary replied politely. 'I do wonder if the source of his feelings is financial, because I made six times more than the rest of Take That,' he said smoothly. 'Robbie needs to get his act together.' (It was true – Gary was thought to have made about £6.5 million because, as songwriter, he was paid royalties. The others probably made about £2.5 million each.) Chris Poole, Robbie's ex-publicist,

summed up the reality. 'If Robbie ad
discipline and Gary had more of Rc
they could both have long, successfu.

As Robbie himself acknowledged, his seu..
inability to keep his mouth shut was actually a way of
understanding everything that had gone on. He was still
finding his feet as a solo artist and still dealing with the
resentments of yesteryear. 'I suppose when you're
feeling whatever emotion you're feeling, you've got to
get it out as catharsis, really,' he said. 'I've done a lot of
slagging off in the press and there hasn't been a lot of
positivity to the people I used to be with.

'To tell you the truth, I'm all over that now. This is
the future. I did an interview the other day and you go
through a time where interviews are like
psychotherapy. Anyway, I was talking about all the lads
and all the good times. Really, that's what I want again
and I wouldn't mind meeting up with them all, but
maybe not the manager! I'd like to meet up with the
manager in a forklift truck, souped up to go about 150
miles per hour, nonstop, with no brakes! I didn't mean
that, honest!'

There were other problems, as well. Ironically, just as
Gary lost two stone and was showing off a new toned
appearance, Robbie's months of bingeing were taking
their toll. He had gained a lot of weight and was no
longer the youthful, slender charmer of before. An
appearance on *TFI Friday* confirmed that, with Robbie
moaning about his triple chins, joking about drinking

Slimfast and being told by Chris Evans, 'It's what's inside and not outside that counts.'

It was something that Robbie was going to have to deal with, not least because he wanted to look his best at the time, and not just so that he could embark on a successful solo career. For Robbie – the Robbie who wasn't interested in long-term relationships, the Robbie who was content with one-night stands with groupies – was about to embark on a whole new phase in his life. Robbie, teen heartthrob turned cool guy, was in love.

5
ROBBIE IN LOVE

Sonia, Lady Colwyn, was rushed off her feet. She had numerous tasks to perform at Witch House, the home in the little village of Gretton in the Cotswolds that she shared with her second husband, John Underwood. Nonetheless, she decided to stop off for a quick glass of white wine at the Bugatti Inn, the village pub, to take the nip off the January cold. Casually sipping away, she turned to the landlady, Jean Grimes, and asked if she had ever heard of someone called Robbie Williams. 'I'd never heard of him myself,' she continued. 'I gather he's some sort of a pop star, apparently.'

He was indeed, Mrs Grimes assured her – quite a famous one, at that. And, while under normal circumstances Sonia would no more take an interest in Robbie Williams than she would the man in the moon, something had happened to spark off her line of enquiry. Robbie was going out with her daughter, the Hon. Jacqueline Hamilton-Smith.

Jacqui, Robbie's first serious girlfriend, could not have been more different from her new amour. The daughter of Sonia and Lord Colwyn, a jazz-loving dentist – 'He drills by day and trills by night' – Jacqui was just seven when her parents divorced, and from then on she divided her time between her mother in Gloucestershire and her father in Chelsea. Sonia came from the family that made the famous Morgan sports cars, while her father, the third Lord Colwyn, came from a family of politicians and soldiers. Jacqui went to school first at the Charlton Park Day School for Girls in Charlton Kings, before moving to a very smart convent school called St Clotild's. Her society connections were impeccable: her father's jazz band provided the music for Prince Andrew's 21st birthday party. Jacqui herself did a bit of modelling and then went on to work as a make-up artist.

Sonia was not best pleased to learn about her daughter's new boyfriend. The two met at a party given by Jacqui's ex-boyfriend, record producer Nellee Hooper, late in 1995, and clicked immediately. Jacqui, at 29 seven years older than Robbie, was soon taking her new beau home to meet the family. Robbie was on his best behaviour, but was quite clearly not what Sonia had in mind as son-in-law material. Asked if she thought the two would marry, she cried: 'Oh good

God, no! He's a lovely boy but that's it. I mean, he's only 22 and I really don't think he would be suitable. No, no, absolutely not. Jacqui meets people in the pop world all the time, but I wouldn't have thought it is the basis for a lasting relationship.'

Lord Colwyn didn't seem best pleased, either. 'It's early days yet,' he said. 'I met Robbie briefly and he seemed a personable enough young man, but neither of them seemed to be thinking in terms of marriage. Jacqui is 29 now and old enough to know her own mind but I don't know how I'd react if they settled down permanently. I mean, since the news got out, I've had endless numbers of teenage girls phoning my office asking if I have Robbie's home telephone number. It's a bit of a bore, frankly, all this fuss.'

Robbie, meanwhile, had taken Jacqui home to meet his own family. Just as Jacqui's lot were unaware that he was quite so famous, Robbie's lot were unaware that she was quite so posh. 'Robbie brought her round, but I had no idea who she was,' said Nan. 'I just said straight out to her, "What's your name, duck?" She was pretty and polite but I had no idea she was aristocracy. It wasn't until I read it in the papers that I realised she was a lady. I nearly had a fit. I felt so embarrassed that I had called her duck.'

Initially, it seemed that this might indeed turn out to be a serious relationship. Jacqui gave Robbie moral support until all the problems with the record company were sorted out, while encouraging him to dress and behave more maturely. They managed to keep it quiet for four months, until they flew to Barbados for a holiday to celebrate Jacqui's 29th birthday, where they stayed in the £300-a-night Coral Reef Club. There, they surfed, snorkelled, played football and revelled in togetherness. 'All I can say is that I'm looking forward to a holiday and a complete rest. I really need it,' said Robbie. 'Jacqueline has been a great support. I just want to be left alone with her. She is a beautiful girl.'

Friends of the couple thought the two might just go the distance, too. Jacqueline is 'Robbie's rock', said one. 'She is very level-headed and down to earth. She is just what he needs.'

Another said that Jacqui had really fallen for Robbie. 'Jacqui has reached the age now where she doesn't just want a relationship for its own sake but is looking for something more,' she said. 'I was very surprised the first time she told me about Robbie, but when you see them together it's obvious they complement one another perfectly.'

Robbie, always eager to share his emotions with the world, was bubbling over with happiness. 'She's posh and bonkers – my perfect woman,' he cried. 'I'm in love for the first time in my life. I had plenty of one-night stands, of course, when I was with Take That but I was never allowed to let anything develop. I'm a 22-year-old man, but until I met Jacqui I had absolutely no idea how to get or keep a real girlfriend. Until then it had always been a case of "Thanks for that and close the door on the way out, will you?" But with Jacqui I knew I wanted something more.'

It seemed he could hardly believe his luck. 'It was the way she said "lovely" in this dead posh accent that got me hooked,' he said, harking back to their first meeting. 'It still does me in now. We talked a lot that night and I fancied her rotten but we didn't see each other again for a few weeks. We were on the phone to each other, though, almost every day. It is a cliché, I know, but something clicked between us. We share the same mad sense of humour and we both love having a good time.'

It was in the company of none other than his new friends, the bad boys, that the relationship initially took off. 'Around November we met up again in Manchester,' Robbie continued. 'Jacqui was in town with her friend Patsy Kensit and I was with Liam Gallagher. The four of us had a great night and there must have been something in the air, because that's when Patsy and Liam got together, as well. Jacqui wasn't looking for a relationship and I certainly wasn't either. I am just a lad from Tunstall but apart from the accent we are frighteningly similar. Jacqui plays down her poshness. She has a job – she works hard as a make-up artist. She spends very little time hunting, shooting and fishing. She never even uses her title. I was the one who insisted we use the names Lord and Lady Tunstall when we checked into the hotel here.'

It was soon after the evening in Manchester that Jacqui

took Robbie home to meet the in-laws. 'As we were driving to the house, I said, "We shan't call this a relationship, shall we?" and she shook her head. The next day I took her to meet my nan in Stoke-on-Trent and, as they sat chatting, it suddenly occurred to me that I was in love. As we got back into the car, I said, "I think this is a relationship after all," and she nodded.'

Even so, it took Robbie some time before he told her he loved her. 'I blame Take That,' he said. 'I can still hear our manager, Nigel Martin-Smith, ordering us not to get involved in a relationship. I had that drummed into me for six years and it was a hard thing to shake off. Nigel would tell us that, if we got involved with a woman, the girls would stop buying our records. It's astonishing I ever managed to sleep with a girl at all because that thought made us so scared. But when Jacqui left Britain a couple of weeks ago to come out to Barbados before me, I found myself feeling sick. I missed her like I had never missed anyone before. When she arrived she phoned me and I just blurted out, "I love you." That was the first time I had ever said that to a woman other than my mum.'

It was impossible not to find Robbie endearing at this stage. He was like a puppy with a new owner: absolutely besotted and determined that everyone, absolutely everyone, would share his joy. If he had been dashing around on a beach wagging his tail, his happiness could not have been more obvious. 'I arrived in Barbados a few days ago and ever since then I have been telling Jacqui I love her about every two minutes,' he went on. 'After six years of not being able to even think about it, now I can't even shut myself up.'

Back in England, the relationship initially seemed to go from strength to strength. The couple moved in together and friends talked about how Jacqui had mellowed Robbie. But old habits die hard and, as his solo career seemed to falter, Robbie took refuge where he always had – in drink and drugs. And this time round it was more serious. Previously, his benders could be seen as a young man reacting against many years of being kept on a leash, but increasingly, it seemed to onlookers, Robbie's drinking was turning into a search for oblivion. 'I'd think, Shit, I should be working,' he once said, 'but then I would go out and get drunk so I didn't have to worry about it. Sometimes, I wouldn't come home for three or four days. There were arguments. And I couldn't tell her I wouldn't do it again because I knew I would. So I just kept saying, "Sorry."'

Matters deteriorated further. Robbie's drinking was getting completely out of control. 'I started to get really unhappy. At one point, I was drinking a bottle of vodka a day,' he said. 'I tried every drug except heroin. I got really fucked up.'

Jacqui had had enough. She told Robbie it was over.

'Jacqui and I have decided to give each other some space,' Robbie said unhappily. 'We are still living in the same house but, yes, we do have some problems that we are trying to work out. You could say that our relationship is in the mire right now. It is fair to say we have split up for the time being but we both hope we can sort out our differences.'

Some hope. Had circumstances been different, perhaps Jacqui might indeed have been the one, for Robbie remained deeply attached to her – some years later, when he discovered she had become engaged to the actor Sean Pertwee, he burst into tears. But at the time, all he was doing was drinking and he could not think clearly about anything else.

'Basically, I'll tell you what happened,' he said a couple of years later. 'When I was in Take That, I used to work my bollocks off. And then, if we got a night off, I'd go out and get pissed. Yeah? As you do. So it all gets on top and I leave the band. Now once you've got no work, my instant think is, go get pissed. So I got pissed – for a year. Longer. Maybe a year and a half, two years. And when the time comes for me to do work again, I'd completely forgotten how to stop drinking. As choreography had been a part of my life, booze was a part of my life. I looked ridiculous. I was saying ridiculous things. And basically I'd got the potential to be one of the biggest artists in the world if I put the work in, looked fine and said good things.'

Very true, but Robbie was not quite there yet. And his excesses were now becoming so public that his family and friends were becoming concerned. Sir Elton John had been through a similar stage and, after watching Robbie drink himself senseless at a party, recommended that he see the well-known celebrity therapist Beechy Colclough, advice that he went on to heed. He also tried for a rapprochement with Jacqui and, although she turned him down, she did say that she would help him through the mess.

Robbie was now cutting a very different figure from that puppy on the beach. He was bloated, invariably either drunk or hung over, and a mess. He knew it, too. 'I've done drugs because I'm insecure,' he said at the time. 'Everybody is screwed up and insecure and it's just a matter of realising it. It's a rebellion, but I'm not proud I've done drugs. I'm against what drugs do to people and the people around them, but if you're on them, fair play.'

A friend put it more succinctly. 'Robbie knows he needs all the help he can get.'

As a backdrop to all this, Robbie was still attempting to establish a solo career. His next manager after leaving Kevin Kinsella was Tim Abbot, who admitted to initial misgivings when he first met Robbie – not least because he came across as a no-hoper. 'Here was this cheeky chappy doing his duck walk, and there was just something about him that was incredibly engaging,' he said. 'I wasn't sure if he was going to be the next George Michael or the next George Formby.' Another rather prescient critic described Robbie as 'more vaudeville than rock 'n' roll'.

It was Abbot who negotiated Robbie's eventual release from RCA and his new deal with Chrysalis but, again, the association did not last long. Robbie sacked him in October 1996, as he was going through yet another low point with Jacqui and drugs: a furious Abbot, like Nigel Martin-Smith and Kevin Kinsella before him, sued Robbie. The gripe was unpaid fees and, ultimately, a couple of years later, Robbie and Tim settled out of court.

At the time, it generated a good deal of bad blood. 'We are extremely disappointed that, despite all our efforts over the past year and the tremendous change in Rob's career we have achieved, he should choose to bring our relationship to an end at such a crucial stage,' said a livid Abbot. 'I would like to think that we could settle the problem of my claim without litigation but I am afraid that it seems inevitable that Rob's lawyers will shortly be hearing from mine. And it seems the whole matter will become subject to the jurisdiction of the courts. It is unfortunate that Rob is now in dispute with three former managers.'

Robbie tried to play it down. 'Basically, I feel it is time to move on,' he said. 'I want total artistic freedom in the creative direction of my album. Tim's been a fantastic help to me over the past months and I know he'll be successful with all the other projects he's working on. We had great success together with the single "Freedom". We haven't fallen out and I know we'll continue to be friends.'

The claim was settled in 1998.

Robbie was beginning to seem out of control. His

solo career still had a long way to go before it really took off, his first real relationship had foundered and, yet again, he was being sued by a manager. (It was at about this time he remarked that he'd been a millionaire three times and lost it three times because of lawsuits.) The bitterness against the other members of Take That had, if anything, become even stronger and, horror of horrors, he was now quite noticeably fat.

'Leaving Take That was a licence to stuff himself silly,' said a friend. 'He revelled in it. He has been starting each day with a gigantic breakfast and his pockets are usually full of chocolate bars. But the real killer is the beer. He adores it. There's a can in his hand at all hours.'

Robbie himself saw his weight gain – up from 11 stone to more than 13 stone – as yet another opportunity for self-loathing. 'I put on weight because it was an anti-Take That thing to do and now I hate myself for it,' he confessed. The stress he was under didn't help, as Robbie ate to gain comfort and drank to forget.

He seemed caught in the most vicious of circles.

Elton John, who had also been addicted to alcohol and cocaine, looked on aghast as he saw Robbie embark on a three-day bender. 'He [Robbie] started on Friday night and finished on Sunday evening, slumped on a friend's floor,' said an onlooker. 'Robbie drank solidly throughout. He can really stick it away and, once he's on a roll, there's no stopping him. Elton says they are very similar characters. He would binge drink for days on end and then collapse into a heap – just like Robbie.'

Beechy Colclough seemed the ideal person to turn to for help. He was used to the problems faced by celebrities, for he had treated not only Elton, but also Michael Jackson and Paul Gascoigne. Elton himself was only too keen to shower his therapist with praise. 'Those of us too proud or too frightened to ask for help need people like Beechy to help us claw our way back into existence,' he said.

Robbie started to lose weight and was pictured going shopping with Sir Elton. A friend summed up the problem. 'He has come through a very dark time. The pressure on him was enormous,' he said. 'But at last there's light at the end of the tunnel. He proved he could make it on his own with his hit "Freedom" and now other top names want to help him on his LP as well. Robbie's had to do his growing up in public, but, by this time next year, he will have made £3 million from a string of hits, as well as having his pick of big film parts and TV presenting offers.'

It was an optimistic appraisal. There was no sign yet of the emergence of a more mature Robbie, and no one was watching his progress with more concern than Jan, Robbie's mother. Ironically, having had to shut down her three dress shops – she was being plagued by Robbie fans – she had just started on a new career as a drugs counsellor. It gave her a unique insight into Robbie's problems.

'Take That gave Robbie a lot of experience, but it also

took away his innocence,' she said in an interview. 'He went in as a child and came out as a man. In the group they were not allowed any opinions. Robbie was told to keep his mouth shut in interviews and not to take away the spotlight from Gary Barlow. He was in denial for such a long time. You can't treat somebody for drink and drug problems until they've addressed the issues themselves. It was only a few weeks ago that he admitted to himself what the rest of us knew, that he was able to get help. I couldn't counsel Robbie as a parent so that's when Elton put him in touch with Beechy Colclough.

'It's lucky Robbie faced up to it so quickly. Some people spend years and years in denial. Now Robbie is more like the son I had before he went into Take That, which, considering all he has gone through, is absolutely fantastic. I'm so proud of him, he's got a new direction, even if it isn't the one he was once heading in. But this has been a difficult time for me, too. Robbie owes me a facelift and a new hair colour for putting me through the worst 12 months of my life.'

Robbie was indeed beginning to behave better. He started playing golf with his mother, and even tried to rekindle the friendship with Mark. Mark had made the first move by slipping a note through Robbie's front door inviting him to tea and biscuits: Robbie took him up on the invitation and went round to listen to his old friend's new disc. Mark was ecstatic. 'We played each other our new songs and it went really well,' he enthused. 'It's as if we'd never been apart. Over the last two weeks I've seen him about four times. He's terrible, though. All he comes over for is dinner and coffee. I haven't been invited to his house yet. He says he's going to have to clean it up first. I'm really pleased we've seen each other. He is still the same old Rob and I'm still the same old me.'

But who was Robbie really? He still gave no indication as to having any idea himself, and lurched into 1997 with, it seemed to observers, no particular game plan. His first public appearance was at, of all things, a Boyzone concert in Dublin in the New Year, when he joined them on stage for an encore. The crowd went wild. 'We love you, Robbie,' they cried, while a spokesman for Boyzone explained, 'Robbie is good friends with the boys and, as he was in Dublin for New Year, we thought it would be a great idea for him to join them for a song. He enjoyed it, but it's not a permanent thing. The fans' reaction shows he's still really popular.'

Robbie was, in fact, in Ireland to celebrate a family Christmas and New Year. The sessions with Beechy were going well and Jan was on hand to look after her errant son. Her pleasure in his new sobriety was obvious. 'I've never seen him looking so happy and so well,' she beamed. 'I'm delighted with the way he's done so much to face up to his problems. Beechy kick-started Robbie and it didn't take him long to get a handle on things again. We've been off for a week in

Dublin and had a very festive, family Christmas. Robert's a young lad and he's intelligent – daft as that might seem to some people. He's been writing a lot of new songs and is desperate to get some records out.'

His management were pleased with his progress, too. 'Robbie's as straight as a die,' said one. 'He's lost weight and is looking good. He's a very young lad and has been through a heck of a lot. People seem to forget he's only 22. He realises he needs discipline. Underneath it all he's a tough bugger.'

He was going to have to be. For a start, his relationship with Jacqui, which had continued intermittently through the autumn, was now completely off, with Jacqui formally wishing Robbie well. Secondly, he was beginning to realise just how tough a fight lay ahead. Work had begun on his first solo album, *Life Thru A Lens* (initially entitled *The Show Off Must Go On*), and it was very important that Robbie established an audience of his own. The music business is a brutal one, and there was no doubt that, if Robbie failed to make it, he would not be allowed a second chance.

Given that he had shown the strength to pull himself out of his drink and drugs phase (part one), the signs were beginning to look good. 'Robbie is going to do really well,' said Peter Lorraine, then editor of *Top Of The Pops* magazine, 'which, knowing how hugely fickle the teenage audience is, isn't something I say lightly. His first single, being a cover, gave you no clues as to what kind of music he was going to make. This time, he has a lot to be proud of: his music is brilliant. And, of course, he was the only one in Take That with any street cred.'

Robbie was beginning to reassess the last year, one that had been largely wasted through his excessive consumption of drink and drugs. 'Five months ago, I wouldn't have been able to do this because of the drink,' he said in an interview. 'And the drugs. I was drinking all day, every day. And taking a lot of coke and Es and speed. But I've been taking drugs since I was 13. I took drugs in Take That – not frequently, but I took everything apart from smack. It's like Frank Skinner said when Brian Harvey got sacked from E17 – "A pop star who does drugs, how unusual."

'But I don't want to involve myself in some big debate here. I wouldn't want anybody to go through what I've done in the last 12 months. You can't win. But when pop stars go on about the perils of drugs, kids look at them and think, Well, you've got the big house and the cars and the girls – it worked for you. All I can say is I didn't like it and I certainly didn't enjoy it and I deluded myself for quite a long time about being so messed up.'

There was no doubt that he was beginning to appreciate his new status, though. He spoke happily about appearing before an audience 'who actually had pubic hair, for once'.

Some habits certainly died hard, though, and one of those was the feud with Gary. They both had new singles out in April 1997, and yet again they were to go head to head. Robbie was to release 'Old Before I Die' on 14 April, while, just two weeks later, Gary was weighing in with a song written by Madonna, 'Love Won't Wait'. The fight was as public and as bitter as ever. 'Gary and Robbie are desperate to show they can achieve as much success by themselves as they did with Take That,' said an industry insider. 'They really want to beat each other at everything – to have the better marketing, better videos and, of course, the better songs.'

In the event, Robbie's single charted at a relatively respectable Number 2. Gary got to Number 1. Again. Robbie kept his head down. He spoke about gaining in confidence and the importance of keeping his weight down – difficult, he said, when you are completely responsible for yourself. He spoke about an interest in Feng Shui. Asked which Spice Girl he would be, he nominated Mel B, aka Scary Spice.

There were signs, though, that Robbie Williams, nutter, was still lurking beneath the surface. As work on the album progressed – by now Robbie was calling it *I Am Not A Pie Eater* – a beard appeared, grown, said Robbie, to cover his double chin. He was clearly still self-conscious about his weight, joking in one interview, 'I won't take the jacket off. I still haven't lost those extra pounds I put on with the birth of my first child.'

He was missing his new friends. 'I don't really see Liam and Patsy any more,' he said regretfully. Back in his flat in

Kensington, close to the Royal Albert Hall, one interviewer noticed a vomit-covered towel. 'It's not mine!' said Robbie hastily. 'It was these two lovely bisexual girls I met in a club. I didn't shag them or anything!' He opened a bottle of red wine. 'You can hear the neighbours shagging' he continued. 'They really go for it. But I'm moving tomorrow – Park Lane or Mayfair or Notting Hill. The removal men are coming at 11am and I'm house-hunting in the afternoon.'

If this was the newly mature Robbie, it left a lot to be desired. Nor did it get much better. Robbie again started reminiscing about his lost weekend, all 18 months of it, except by this time it was beginning to appear as a boast. 'Hey, right, you'll love this, right,' he went on. 'I'm on a yacht with Al Fayed and some royal people and it's dead swish. All the food's downstairs, and I'd not had my pie ration for the day, so I go down for a look at the running buf-fay. But the steps in boats are dead steep, they're just bang bang bang bang like a ladder. I fell the length of those stairs, arse over tit, and wind up in a heap at the feet of all these posh people. They're like, "Oh, the pop star Johnny's arrived."'

Another of the great and good to enjoy Robbie's presence was Bono. 'He's dead intense,' said Robbie. 'You meet him and he devotes all his attention to you, focuses on your face and asks you loads of questions. He's really interested. It's like, You Are Talking To Bono. I stayed in his castley-housey thing and in the bogs he's got all these photographs. Pictures of, say, the Bosnian prime minister, with a huge handwritten note next to it about how much he enjoyed meeting Bono and all that. Prime ministers, presidents, everything, all with these notes. So I'm sat on the bog thinking, I should leave something, too. Some kind of note or a letter or something. In the end, I just wrote, "To Bono, love Robbie." I might have put a kiss on it too. I was too pissed to remember, to be honest.'

And with that, Robbie enthused about his new album, complained about his treatment at the hands of the music industry and terminated the interview when he was reminded the removal men were due the next day. 'Ah, fuck that,' he said. 'To tell you the truth, if you go, I'll be bored. Do you want to come out drinking?'

6
YEAH, I'M A BIT OF A SLAG

As Robbie coped with the humiliation of having come second to Gary for the second time, he slid right back to where he had been a few months earlier. Out went sobriety, in came the birds and the booze, with the actress Anna Friel the first woman Robbie was seen out with. He then promptly ditched her and went off with someone else. Although in the years to come he categorically denied having had a romance with Anna, at the time he played it up for all it was worth.

'Yeah, I'm a bit of a slag,' he said cheerfully in an interview after coming round from a 72-hour bender, much of it spent in the company of a blonde with a seahorse tattoo on her breast. 'I think to myself, Well, I'm young so what does it matter? But some people don't like it if you're a slag. They say it's not nice. Well, I'm 23 and I've got hormones and it's there, so why not?

If you're a slag and you're a man, your mates think it's great. You're seen as brilliant. But if a girl is a slag, it's totally different by society's standards. It's completely hypocritical and that's wrong. Sex is good. Everybody does it and everybody should.'

In an increasingly rambling interview, after which Robbie went off for yet another spell in rehab, it soon emerged that something else had made its way back into his life, too: drugs. 'There's obviously a euphoria attached to drugs,' he said. 'My experience of them is that at first you've got your hands in the air dancing in a club and you feel fucking great and the world is fucking great and everything is brilliant. And then 12 months down the line, when you're just caning it, your arms start to come down and you say to yourself the euphoria has gone. It's not working any more.

'The hard thing is actually realising when you are in trouble. People worry about you and ask how you are. And you say, "I'm fine, I'm fine. I'll just carry on as I am." You carry on with drugs, even though things are falling apart. You say to yourself, "I have not got a problem with this." But, before you know it, you have. I don't think you can go through frequent drug taking and then have the sense to take leave of it. I don't think I personally could. I don't have a switch which I can turn on or turn off in my head. If I do something, I really go for it, which is unfortunate in a case like this. If you say you can take it or leave it, you are still continuing to take drugs and probably

YEAH, I'M A BIT OF A SLAG

just kidding yourself that you can give up when you want. You say to yourself, "I can handle it tomorrow, which is a lie to yourself."'

He then proceeded to announce that the Pope should try cannabis. 'It's just a quirky thing,' he said. 'I just wonder what it would be like to see the Pope on drugs. It would be nice. Can you imagine him with a joint in his hand when he blesses people? Instead of incense in church, there would be a smell of a spliff.' Robbie Williams, nutter, had clearly taken leave of the plot.

And it was downhill from there. Whether it was from a lack of personal direction or simply a lack of willpower, Robbie was thrashing around out of his depth yet again, with all the inherent danger of finally going under. As before, friends and family were desperately concerned, while not quite knowing what to do. It was becoming clear that Robbie's first descent into drink and drugs was not a one-off, rather a sign of a deep depression that has plagued him throughout his adult life.

'The Robbie you read about is not the real Robbie,' said a close friend who had known him for years. 'He's very misunderstood, and half of what is said about him – or even by him – isn't true. He is basically a good kid who has been famous his entire adult life and has become screwed up as a result. He's not this wild, debauched, drug-crazed pop star people imagine him to be. He's a lonely, insecure lad with a kind heart who's had a lot to deal with. Yes, when he goes out he overdoes things, but he's not constantly out of his mind. His pop star persona is grossly exaggerated. Any problems Robbie has come down to one thing and one thing only: he's depressed, and moving to London has only made matters worse for him.'

While much of this was undoubtedly true, there was one other element that might well have contributed to his depression, both then and now: his failed relationship with Jacqui. While Robbie went on to become briefly engaged to another woman and has also announced he's never really been in love, he clearly was utterly besotted with Jacqui at the time. Indeed, some people believe he has never really got over her, hence his sometimes callous treatment of other women and his inability to find a long-term relationship. And while it was the drugs that soured Robbie's relationship with Jacqui, the end of that relationship, in turn, might well have turned him back on them.

And, of course, his history with Take That and his abrupt sacking from the group continued to cast a very long shadow. 'Robbie went straight from school to travelling the world with Take That,' said a member of the group's former entourage. 'He had been looked after and cosseted to such a degree that he became almost dysfunctional without them. He was returned to the real world not knowing what the real world was and, because he was away from home so much during his time with the group, he lost touch with a lot of people. Leaving the group was like coming out of prison, in a way, because everyone had moved on and he was on his own.

'He had no management, no guidance and very few true friends left. Those who count themselves as true friends will tell you that they only really hear from him when things get tough. The fair-weather friends he made in London and through his relationship with Jacqui were superficial and only attracted to his fame, and he knows that. But he is a very trusting person and he hates being on his own. He is happy to indulge these people because all they want to do is drink with him and go to parties and that helps him to forget his problems. But he always hates himself at the end of it.'

Poor Robbie. He might have had the typical rock star's habits, but he had none of the typical rock star's enjoyment of those habits and, yet again, he had taken it too far. Despite attempting to make a joke of it – 'They say the sure sign someone is an alcoholic is when they drink first thing in the morning. I never did that – but only because I was always unconscious until early afternoon!' – he was well aware that he had let the side down. 'Robbie knew that he would be going into treatment the following week and let himself go,' said his spokesman. 'But he's not making any excuses. He's deeply ashamed of himself and it has made him all the more determined to get himself sober.'

And so, off Robbie went for a six week detoxifying treatment. 'Robert is poorly. He has a drink problem but he's been looking at the whole situation for 12 months now and doing it of his own free will,' said his weary mother. 'I love him like any mum would love her son and you do what you can. I know Robert will be all right. I'm proud of him. The whole situation from Take That to right now has been a major contribution to his problem.'

His record company, Chrysalis, which cannot have been pleased by the turn of events, issued a statement saying it was 'entirely supportive of any decision Robbie may have taken regarding his own wellbeing. We believe Robbie is, without a doubt, a great talent and he has the depth and diversity to become the brightest star of his generation. We are delighted with the as yet unmixed songs which have been filtering out of the studio and predict the album contains many singles which will drive the campaign through into 1998.'

Beechy Colclough issued a statement to the effect that he had absolutely no idea what was going on.

It didn't help that, although his court case with RCA had been settled, Robbie was still being sued by Nigel Martin-Smith for unpaid commission and was due in court that July. His behaviour continued to be bizarre. In one gesture of defiance, he was photographed giving a V for victory sign as he posed in an Alfa Romeo sports car for the cover of his new album. 'It's his way of showing the court case won't get him down,' said a friend.

The case began and Robbie was caught nipping out for a cigarette. 'I don't even want to be here,' he declared. 'I should be sunning myself in the park. But after this I'm off to become a member of the clergy. I'm serious. I'm off to India to become a priest.'

The case finally revealed to the world what had really happened when Robbie left the band. It emerged that it was Gary and Jason who were particularly upset by Robbie's behaviour and were concerned that he was alienating the fans. Mark, meanwhile, was 'close to collapse'. By 1994, Robbie had developed 'a taste for glamorous company, narcotics and alcohol'. He was turning up to work 'hung over and unable to rehearse'. And so it went on. Robbie lost the case, but said he would appeal.

Meanwhile, his solo career continued to fail to set the world on fire. Robbie's next single, 'Lazy Days', the third on his own and also released that July, only made it to Number 8. And Robbie's own description of the track said a lot about his own recent activities. 'Well, actually, it's strange because it's all about being drunk,' he said in a radio interview. 'It's about, you know, that feeling that you get when you've got a bottle of wine and it's a sunny day and you're underneath a tree with a person – the woman, the man that you love. It's nothing about that whatsoever! It's just about sex and drink!'

Certainly Robbie was still feeling negative about relationships. 'At this moment, I don't think I'm a one-woman-type of guy,' he confessed. 'I'm probably going to regret making that comment for the rest of my life. But it's like marriage – I can't ever see myself tying the knot. Maybe I need to spend some nights with a lot more women. Then I might finally have the incentive to settle down.'

But, at least now that he was out of rehab again, Robbie was beginning to look more in control. He had lost weight, had a new haircut and seemed back on course. He had met other people with stories to tell and had even gone running every morning at 6am in an effort to reclaim reality. 'The time in the clinic was hell,' he proclaimed, open as always about his life. 'I had to undergo a strictly planned routine. At the beginning, I wasn't even allowed out of my room. Nobody was allowed to visit me – apart from my mother. It was like in prison and you're thinking everybody out there has forgotten you.'

They hadn't, by any means, but this was not the last time he was to end up in rehab and he was still a long way from pulling himself out of the mire. 'Yesterday I didn't have a drink and today I probably won't have a drink,' he proclaimed. 'And that's good enough for me.' And of the future? 'I can't promise that I won't do it. I'm only human. I'm imperfect.'

But the experience had clearly chastened him. Robbie might have been self-indulgent, but he was not stupid, and he clearly realised he was close to being in real trouble. 'It was this lovely house in Wiltshire, loads of cows outside and me and loads of other drug addicts,' he said. 'It's a very humbling experience, very powerful, the hardest thing I've had to do in my life and the most rewarding. The thing in England is about this stiff upper lip thing where we're not allowed to show our feelings. Even though we're running around being really vulnerable and putting defences up it's, "Oh, he's more fucked up than us – he's gone to see a counsellor."

'Of course, when you go to rehab it's, "Fucking hell! He must be fucked up!" But, seeing what goes on there, I'd actually send my kids there as a finishing school. I really would. It's like going and having your head cleaned for a bit.'

It finally seemed to be getting through to Robbie, though, that, if he was to have a long-term career as a solo artist, he was going to have to start taking it a bit more seriously. 'This is work,' he said. 'This is what you do. I realise that now. Everything's scary at the moment. I'm scared about everyday living. I seem to have acquired nerves from somewhere.'

As September approached, Robbie prepared for the release of *Life Thru A Lens*, his first solo album. A lot was riding on it. History and the music business are not kind to those they perceive to be failures and, if Robbie wanted to avoid the legions of solo artists with a brilliant future behind them, he had to make this album sell. And still his career seemed to be on the verge of stalling: his fourth single, 'South Of The Border', was out in the same month and did even worse than its predecessors. It managed a limp Number 14 in the charts, to date Robbie's least successful single ever.

The temptation to go on another binge to forget about it all was enormous, but for once Robbie managed to stay sober – for now, at least. Apart from anything else, he realised that his endless drinking was causing his mother a great deal of anxiety and pain – and Robbie, whatever his other faults, has never underestimated her importance in his life. In fact, he dedicated a song on the album to her. 'I wanted to apologise so, as soon as I wrote "One Of God's Better People", I took my guitar up to Newcastle-under-Lyme and played it to her,' he said. 'When she heard it, she just sat there and cried. I think it's the line "It must hurt you to see your favourite man lose himself again and again" that did it. But no matter how caned I got, I never lost sight of how much she means to me and things are great between us now.'

And Robbie was going through yet another bout of self-re-assessment. Yet again he was using interviews as a form of therapy and yet again he was revealing quite how excessive his lifestyle had become. 'The thing about drugs and sex is that you lose all your inhibitions,' he admitted. 'I had sex in trains, planes, restaurants and wine bars. Oh, and in car parks. I had sex in car parks quite a lot. It wasn't Anna Friel – we were just friends. I choose the wrong women. People expect a pop star to have a model girlfriend when actually they're more fucked up than me! I would like the whole wife and family thing one day – but only when the time's right. You probably won't believe this but, behind everything, I'm a real loner. It's been the same ever since I was a kid and it's something I've got to work on.'

Robbie was also beginning to realise the need to differentiate between his private and public lives. He had often said that moving to London might have been a big mistake and, although he had by now settled down and intended to stay, he needed a private place in which to recover from the toll taken by – as he himself put it – life through a lens. 'I know it sounds brutal, but I think it's sad when fans turn up from Italy and camp on my doorstep,' he said. 'I'd never invite them inside like Liam and Noel. Good on 'em if they give handouts but it's an invitation for thousands of them to do it now. My home is my only bastion. If you want to come and see me, come to a gig.'

Publicly, Robbie was professing himself to be unconcerned about his new album's performance. 'If the album bombs, I couldn't give a toss,' he claimed. 'I'm proud of it. Besides, I can always go into TV.' But underneath it all, he was well aware of the fact that it had to do well. 'It will be interesting to see what musical pigeonhole people try to put me in,' he admitted. 'The music is a big change from Take That. People may have difficulty liking it because it's me, but I love what I've done. It's fantastic.'

Given Robbie's tendency to wear his heart on his sleeve and reveal absolutely everything about his inner life at any given moment, it was also unsurprising that the album had a strong autobiographical element. Robbie was aware of that. 'My lyrics are really personal, but that's just the way I write,' he said. 'Anyway, so much of my private life is on display, why should I worry? Then again, there are times when I think I should be more guarded about what I say to people. When I was in Take That, everything was controlled and we were very careful about what we did and said. I'm not like that now, you may have noticed!'

Preparations were also afoot for a tour to support the album. Again, there was a certain degree of nervousness in the industry. While Robbie was undoubtedly a crowd puller and a performer, in the past he had always had the other four members of Take That on stage with him: now he had to show that he could carry the show alone. Robbie professed to be totally relaxed about the ordeal ahead. 'I'm really looking forward to it,' he said. 'The really great thing about this time is that nothing is scripted, it'll be different every night. Not even I know what will happen when I get behind the microphone. I've been working hard enough – ironic as my last single was "Lazy Days". Every spare moment I get is taken up with writing the second album – I don't want to stop. I had a good couple of years going off to parties, doing what I wanted, now it's time to work. I've just discovered I'm in the best industry in the world.'

And one that still contained Gary Barlow. Asked if he felt competitive towards Gary, he replied, 'No, not really ... er, yes, I do.' He went out and bought Gary's first solo album, and then returned it to the shop, loudly asking for a refund because he thought it was 'shit'. He admitted to feeling animosity towards the other members of Take That. The wounds, though healing, had clearly run deep.

And, despite the romance with Jacqui and the legions of women since, questions were again arising about the real nature of Robbie's sexuality. He himself was partly to blame. Whether as a joke or because he was genuinely confused, Robbie himself fuelled the rumours as much as anyone. On one occasion, he was asked how comfortable he was with his sexuality.

'I'm really comfortable with my sexuality,' he replied. 'I could sleep with a bloke today. But I actually don't want to. I might do it tomorrow. I've no qualms. It's just not something I've wanted to do. But I might do. I'll probably dabble before I die. But it's like people think: It [Take That] was only camp as Christmas because there was a gay impresario behind it and that was his vision of macho men. It couldn't fail to be anything other; it's a boy band, for goodness sake. Boy bands are camp. But then so is Bobby Gillespie, Jarvis Cocker, Vic Reeves ... I suppose it's a vaudevillian thing. Indie bands do the shy and coy thing and that's real. They're doing the real thing where they're shy and coy. But I'm an extrovert and that is invariably camp. If you use expressions and you use your hands, you're gonna be camp.'

For what it is worth, Robbie is not gay or even bisexual. One of the trainers at Club Kensington, the gym at which Robbie works out to this day, describes the interest with which he views the women who come to use the gym.

And so, the album was released and the tour kicked off. To everyone's enormous relief, both were very well received, partly as a result of Robbie's own persona. 'I am not sure that people care about the music,' said Neil Mason of *Melody Maker*. 'There is the myth of Robbie Williams. He is good value. A cheeky, fun chap stuck on an album is going to be all right. It's not going to fail.'

Kate Thornton, a former editor of *Smash Hits*, agreed. 'What he has over the others is being a born entertainer,' she said. 'In the last two years, his solo career has produced some very mature pop. He has matured massively as a performer and as a writer. Any great album has to come from the heart and it's brave of him to put all of this on record. It's like signing off that part of his life. What he has said in his songs is nothing that hasn't been said in public.'

It was clear that Robbie had lost none of his ability to charm the public. Natalie Cambrook, a great fan of the star, recalls meeting him just as his solo tour got under way. 'When I met Robbie it was 2 October 1997, the second night of his first solo tour,' said Natalie, who was

16 at the time and is now a writer. 'He had played at the Southampton Guildhall and me and my friend, Lucy, decided to follow his tour bus after the concert. We were avid Take That fans and used to follow them all round the country. There was a certain network of fans who used to trace where they were, which hotel they'd be staying in, which restaurant they'd be going to, and so on, and we used to share information within the network, so we knew their exact movements all the time. It was all top secret and we'd only share it with certain people. Someone always knew someone in the town where they were next playing, working in the hotel they were checked into or whatever. Then we'd check into the same hotel at the same time.

'Anyway, back to Robbie. For years we had followed Take That and we would be in one of an army of cars following the tour bus. We got ready, as we always did, to follow it, by leaving the concert early during the encore to get the car ready, because they'd always leave immediately to avoid being mobbed. As usual, Robbie was whisked away within seconds. It became apparent pretty much straight away that we were the only car following, which had never happened before. We knew from previous information that Robbie would be staying in London that night, so we were all set to follow him there with the hope of meeting him when he got off the coach in the middle of the night at the other end, or possibly if they stopped at a service station on the way.

'I remember the feeling of excitement driving down the M3 knowing that we were the only ones behind and I had a feeling that tonight would be the night, so to speak. I'd never met Robbie before. I'd met all the others, but never Robbie. We were just about to pass Junction 11 of the M3 at Winchester (I remember it so well!) when the coach started to veer from one side of the road to the other and was leaking oil. It pulled on to the hard shoulder, so, obviously, so did we. The coach driver knew we were following but we never really knew whether the band did because the coach was always blacked out.

'Anyway, we sat there for a few minutes deciding what to do, when the coach driver got out and came and asked us if we had any spare oil. We didn't and he went back to the coach. We sat there deciding what to do next when out of the shadows of the coach on the grass verge appeared Robbie. I remember my heart leaping to my throat and my mouth going dry. I couldn't believe my eyes: there in front of me on the hard shoulder of the M3 at 1am was Robbie Williams – and he was coming towards our car. I remember instinctively grabbing Lucy's hand and we sat there holding hands, so nervous we could hardly breathe. We said over and over, "What do we do? What do we do?" All the while he was getting closer and closer. Then we decided we could offer him a lift – anything to make conversation.

'Meanwhile, he was staring straight into the car, so Lucy wound down her window and he made for her side of the car (the driver's side). She was right against the edge of the motorway so he couldn't stand there because there were cars whizzing past, so he went round the front of the car to my side. I began to unwind my window as I saw him coming, but he came right round and opened the door and – I'll remember the words forever – said, "Budge up!" Now this was an E-reg Ford Fiesta, so there was hardly any room, but I moved over as far as I could and he got in. He finished his cigarette and stubbed it out and then shut the door so there was Robbie and me on the passenger seat of a Ford Fiesta.

'I remember him telling us they were sending another coach for him, but I don't remember word-for-word what he said because I was so overwhelmed by his presence. This was post-druggie Robbie – he had stopped drinking so much, lost the weight he gained after leaving Take That, no longer had bleached blonde hair but a shaved head again, and was really back on form. I was basically sitting on his knee and, while Lucy could shift round in her seat and look at him, I was a little in front of him and practically cheek to cheek, so I couldn't look into his face as much as she could. I could only see when he was actually talking to me, if that makes any sense. I remember looking down and seeing how big his hands were and how muscly his legs were – they were rock hard!! I have a vivid memory of his smell which enveloped me immediately – consumed both of us. But by far my most vivid memory is his green eyes. They were so startling and clear and when he looked at you they bore right into you. His skin was completely clear and you could see the pores on his face but it was the eyes that entranced me the most.

'He is by far the sexiest man I have ever met and with a presence that takes your breath away. I now know the true meaning of the word star-struck and that was it. For years he had been smiling out of the posters on my bedroom walls and I'd watched him on TV, listened to his music and seen him in concert, but nothing prepared me for THAT. He sat with us in the car until the other coach arrived and we chatted about all sorts of things. He was particularly interested in what we thought of the concert and asked us all sorts of questions. It was only the second night of his first tour so I guess he wanted to know the reaction.

'We went through practically every song he'd performed and he asked this and that – I remember him listening intently to everything we said. He told us how he was feeling about going solo and how he was worried about putting on weight again because the only thing for him to eat after the show that night had been pizza and that on tour that was always the way, there was no routine. That was it really. He left us completely spellbound on the hard shoulder of the M3 wondering whether we'd been dreaming.

'During this time we'd had the hazard warning lights on, as obviously it was dark, and when we went to start the engine the battery was flat! So we had to call out the Green Flag and when the bloke arrived to jumpstart the car I think he thought we were mad. We told him we'd just met Robbie Williams but I don't think he believed us! All I can say is that as a teenage heartthrob, the first man I fell in love with, he lived up to every expectation and more. He was funny, sexy, concerned that we'd followed him all that way, grateful we'd enjoyed the show (as if we wouldn't) and he actually thanked us for supporting him. He was interested in everything we had to say and there was so much HE wanted to ask US!'

There was the odd stunt that backfired. In October, he upset some fans by leaving the stage at the Manchester Academy, stripping off then returning to sing a final song in the nude, before mooning at the crowd instead of bowing and disappearing off into the night. Not everyone was impressed. There was also yet another public go at Gary Barlow, when Robbie announced that the song 'Ego-A-Gogo' was always assumed to be about his old band member – 'I don't know why.'

Unbelievably, given the history between them, Robbie and Gary actually appeared together in December 1997, at Princess Diana's Concert of Hope. Appearing in front of 6,000 fans at Battersea Power Station in South London, the two hugged and joked on stage together, after which they joined the other performers at the concert in an emotional rendition of The Beatles' 'Let It Be'. 'It was great to see Rob again,' said Gary. 'As soon as I saw him I just went over and hugged him. It's great to be working together again for such a good cause.'

The hatchet was buried, temporarily, at least. As for Robbie, he performed six numbers at the concert, including his latest single, which he dedicated to the late Princess. That single was to establish him as a massive star in his own right, and went on to become one of the all-time pop classics. It was called 'Angels'.

7

HE'S THE ONE – AND SO IS SHE

Guy Chambers was in a rut. His career was going nowhere and the 33-year-old singer/songwriter was seriously beginning to wonder what he would do next. It was at this point that serendipity struck. Guy had given Paul Curran of BMG Publishing a showreel of his music; Curran had it biked round to IE Management. IE, run by David Enthoven and Tim Clark, were and are looking after Robbie and were looking for a songwriting partner for their young protégé. At exactly the same time, a friend of Robbie's mother Jan told IE about a marvellous singer/ songwriter she had heard of: one Guy Chambers. It was almost as if fate was taking a hand.

Robbie and Guy met and took to one another instantly. And it didn't come a moment too soon for Guy. 'When I met Rob, I was at a pretty low point and that was what saved me,' he said. 'I can't underestimate that in my life. I was living in a little flat in Archway and it was a complete shithole. I was fucking up.'

Although a relatively unknown name, Guy was already a music business veteran. He had replaced Karl Wallinger in the band The Waterboys, but it didn't work out. 'I got thrown out of The Waterboys when they went to Dublin,' he said. 'I wanted to collaborate and Mike Scott wasn't having any of that. So he sent me home.' The next stop was World Party, which Guy joined in 1986 at Wallinger's invitation. Five years later, he left that, too. 'He [Wallinger] didn't take my songs very seriously,' said Guy. 'I'd play him a song but he'd go, "Yeah, it's all right, but it's just pop rubbish." So I left and formed my own band, The Lemontrees.'

He didn't find success there, either. The Lemontrees released one album and were promptly dropped by their label, Parlophone. It was then that his name cropped up in conjunction with Robbie. 'Rob didn't know who I was,' said Guy. 'He saw my name on a list of 10 writers – and I was about number six down – and he just liked the look of my name. He didn't know who World Party were, he was just into hip hop and Frank Sinatra. I bought my first flash pad the following year.'

It certainly looked like fate to Robbie. 'The record company gave me a list of people I might like to work with,' he said. 'They read these names out and I went, "Him". I didn't know anything about Guy, it was a spiritual thing. It was like a voice inside my head telling me to pick him. And it's worked. It's dead weird really, but I just knew his name sounded right.'

The pairing bore fruit almost immediately. Robbie had an idea about where he wanted to go, but, pre-Guy, had no one to take him there. All that changed at once. 'I think for Rob that it was like writing with a big brother,' said Chris Briggs of EMI. 'Guy's much more phlegmatic than Rob and they took very different routes to where they are now: Rob joined a boy band for a laugh; where Guy was serious, educated, middle-class, musically trained. But they got together in a little Holloway studio and the songs started to flow.'

They certainly did. Robbie was the poppy lyrics half of the duo, whereas musically trained Guy wrote the music. And they were not afraid to find inspiration anywhere they could. 'We've always tried to plunder the best bits of modern music,' Guy once said. 'Rob has never put his hand up and claimed to be the most original artist on the planet, but there's a strong argument to say he's the most entertaining.'

Robbie was over the moon about his new friend. 'It's funny, because last year I went around saying, "Writing songs is easy,"' he said in an interview in 1997. 'I made out I had loads of songs, and I hadn't. I was lying. I kept saying, "I'm brilliant, me," and I wasn't really. By the beginning of this year I was pretty worried about what I was going to do. Then this person called Guy Chambers walked into my life and he helped turn things around.

The songs just started flowing out and I wrote the album in six days!'

Exactly who had done the most work on the tracks is open to debate. In latter years, as Robbie grew ever more successful, he became increasingly annoyed when anyone suggested Guy's input was crucial and, indeed, the two parted company in 2002, of which more later. But back at the beginning, Robbie was happy to let his new friend receive the credit, admitting that he would turn up at the studio to lay down his lyrics and leave the rest to Guy and his musicians. 'I trust them implicitly,' he said. 'A typical song is done in four takes. If it takes any longer, I'm bored. I don't wanna be there.'

It took a little while for the rest of the world to catch on to the new partnership, and the duo's first three singles together were unremarkable. But the fourth, 'Angels', released at the end of 1997, marked a complete turning point in Robbie's career.

'Angels' actually came about from Robbie's 1996 trip to Dublin, where he met musician Ray Heffernan in a bar, and embarked on a drinking session, before crashing at his house and starting to write what was to be his biggest hit. The pair recorded Robbie singing some of the lyrics on an old Dictaphone, while Ray strummed away on his acoustic guitar. Later, Guy added a chorus, and the rest is history.

In many ways 'Angels' summed up the mood of the nation at the time. At the end of August that year, the country, and indeed the world, had been shocked to the

Robbie beams in a St Margaret Ward High School photo, around 1990.

om left: Born to perform. Robbie (*back left*) when he appeared in *Chitty Chitty Bang* for the Stoke on Trent Drama Company in 1985.

om right: Slim before he was winning, a young Williams shows that unmistakeable grin.

Top: Robbie at eight with his Dad (*left*). Robbie had issues with his father, but here (*right*) they kiss and make up on stage before he performs his new single 'Feel' on *Top Of The Pops*.

Bottom: Early Take That photocalls. The group caused an international storm, though later Robbie compared being in the band to working in your favourite shop but havi to 'clean up the dog turd outside'.

e people worried that Robbie was taking ecstasy when he started appearing in public
:ing a dummy, a common activity among party people in the nineties.

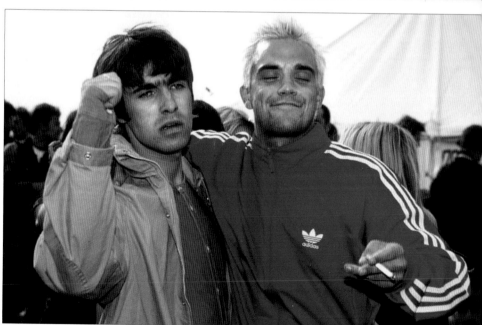

Top: Robbie may have been 'Legless!' at the Brits in 1999, but it didn't stop him think up a new use for his award.

Bottom: Robbie hangs out with Liam Gallagher at Glastonbury. Today they couldn't I further apart.

e (a look at) that. Robbie's lost weekend in Glastonbury infuriated his fellow band
nbers, and gave him more street cred than he could ever have hoped for in a boy band.

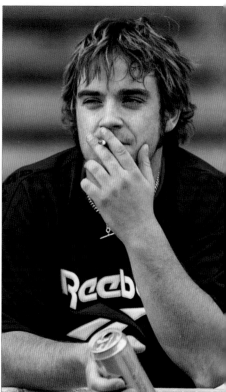

Back in the days before giving up alcohol, Robbie was renowned for his partying on and off the pitch. Here he models his blacked out tooth at Glastonbury, and relaxes with a beer and a fag during the Music Industries Soccer Six Tournament. Here, (*bottom*) he clutches a bottle of champagne on a night out in London.

Top: Nobody really knows how spicy Robbie's relationship with former Spice Girl Geri Halliwell was, but their holidays and public appearances together caused huge speculation.

Bottom: Robbie is pictured in Hollywood attending his weekly alcoholics anonymous meeting. Geri accompanied him and waited patiently outside with a canine friend.

Top: Prince Charming. Robbie meets Prince Charles with Geri to celebrate The Prince of Wales's 50th Birthday.

Bottom: A less royal mess. Robbie enjoys a food fight with Patsy Kensit on her birthda

core by the sudden and unexpected death of Diana, Princess of Wales. The 36-year-old Princess was at the height of her beauty and popularity, and her death in a road accident seemed at the time quite as horrifying as the assassination of John F Kennedy.

Although 'Angels' was not written with Diana in mind, it seemed to encapsulate what everyone felt, with its constant refrain 'I'm loving angels instead'. And when Robbie dedicated it to Diana at the memorial concert, its fate was sealed. Although it only got to Number 4, 'Angels' became a massive hit, Robbie's biggest as a solo artist, and one of the most popular songs of the decade. It spent 13 weeks in the Top Ten, while Robbie won round a whole new group of fans by singing the song live on *Top Of The Pops*.

And if that were not enough, Robbie appeared on *Parkinson* and openly discussed his battles with drink and drugs. It cemented his reputation as the nation's favourite tearaway, and the BBC was inundated with calls offering support. 'Robbie is everyone's favourite bad boy,' said one BBC executive. 'Mums like him just as much as their daughters and the boys like him too, because he likes football and doesn't seem to take the whole thing too seriously. He's a star turn and the BBC are doing everything to persuade him to think of diversifying into television.'

'Angels' did something else, as well: it boosted sales of *Life Thru A Lens*. When it was released in September, it hadn't done massively well and Robbie had admitted to some concern. 'Yeah, I am disappointed and, yeah, it does worry me a bit,' he said. 'But I don't want to see success or failure in terms of sales; it's to do with the quality of the music. I love what I do and I want to be a pop star but, if it doesn't work out in music, there's a place for me somewhere else, entertaining in a different way. The most important thing is that I've done a wicked album and a brilliant tour. I don't care whether people love it or hate it – I just don't want people to think it's nice. No one is ever going to say my concert is nice. They'll either say I rock or I suck. Which is fine by me!'

In the event, there was no need to worry: a couple of months after its release, the album finally took off. Robbie celebrated in his own inimitable fashion: he fell first for a new woman and then off the wagon. The woman in question was, of all unlikely candidates, Mel C of the Spice Girls, then at the height of their popularity. Known to all as Sporty Spice, Mel had recently swapped her tracksuits for some all-out glamour. Robbie was, temporarily, hooked.

'Melanie fancied Robbie when she first met him at a showbiz party but neither wanted to make a move,' said an onlooker. 'They exchanged numbers and started ringing each other nearly every day. When they were both in London last month, they decided they should meet up – and Melanie realised that Robbie felt the same about her. They find it hard to see each other as often as they want with their busy lives, but they are making a huge effort. Whenever their schedules let them, they meet up. When David Beckham flew to France to see Victoria last month, Mel was jetting out of France to see Robbie.'

In the event it was only to be a quick fling, but Robbie and his entourage had other problems on their mind. In early January 1998, Robbie went for a quick drink in London's exclusive Groucho Club, a quick drink that turned into a marathon bender. 'He was smashed,' said a member of the party. 'His eyes were rolling in his head as he was carried out.'

The usual round of apologies and recriminations began. Jan, Robbie's mother, was not best pleased. 'She was very disappointed,' said a friend of the family. 'Robbie admitted drinking but swore he hadn't touched drugs. He said he thought that, after being clean for six months, he could have the occasional drink without losing control. But Friday night has been a very painful reminder for him that he is an alcoholic.'

Robbie was sulky. 'Yes, I had a few drinks,' he said. 'Who wouldn't if your album just went shooting back into the album charts, but it was all in moderation.'

The album was certainly doing well. After that initial lull, the success of 'Angels' was propelling it ever higher, eventually to land at the Number 1 slot (just as Gary's first album, *Open Road*, did). And Chrysalis, part of EMI, was exasperated by the bad press. 'Why can't people just forget all that stuff from the past and write about the fact that he's healthy and doing fantastically well now?' complained a spokesman. It was hard, of course, when Robbie himself kept providing such good copy, not least by stripping off in public so often.

'It's because I always used to do it as a kid!' he explained. 'It's a habit I haven't grown out of! Is it a publicity stunt? No way! I stripped at the end of my gig in Manchester because I was hot. It wasn't to get publicity. It's just a rock 'n' roll thing to do. And why not? I enjoy getting my kit off. I prefer having no clothes on. I walk around the house naked, I'm more comfy that way. Someone wrote a review of the gig saying, "Anyone who has to take their clothes off as a publicity stunt is in trouble." That's rubbish!'

Everything Robbie did was beginning to attract attention. It emerged that one of the songs on his album, 'Hello, Sir', was written to get back at a teacher who told him he would go nowhere. 'I am the boy you reduced to tears, the kid who would not amount to much,' he sang. The *Daily Express* tracked down the teacher mentioned in the song and found Steve Cartlidge, who had taught Robbie English in his final year.

'I merely gave Robbie some sound career advice,' said a clearly amused Cartlidge. 'I told him that entering showbusiness was all very well, but he should first concentrate of getting qualifications and passing his exams. I am treating Robbie's poem light-heartedly. I am actually a fan of his music. One of his songs is absolutely superb. My wife buys his singles, but my own taste favours light pop music like the Eagles and the Doors.

'Although he seems to be a very angry young man, I am sure if we met we would get on famously. Robbie should call and meet me some time and we could have a drink together. Nowadays, I use Robbie as an example to engender ambition in children I teach. I tell them that if their hearts are set on a particular career, then they should go for it – and never mind the advice of a tired old English master.

'Robbie must be a late developer, because the English he uses in his song lyrics is very impressive – well worth marks of grade C or above. My message to him would be, "I am truly happy that you are so successful. Your latest work is very impressive. Good luck."'

Nor was Robbie exactly low profile when it came to his romantic life. The fling with Mel C over, he was young, free and single again – and about to embark on his second serious relationship. It was a cold night in January when Robbie joined a host of A-list stars to sing at the Noel Coward Tribute concert, in the hopes of raising £1 million to combat AIDS. Also on the bill were the girl group All Saints, currently at Number 1 with the single 'Never Ever' and talked of (erroneously) as successors to the Spice Girls.

One in particular caught Robbie's eye: Nicole Appleton, who he had met briefly once before. The two spent much of the night in conversation before leaving together in a limo. Were they an item? No one was saying, but Robbie had spoken in a recent interview about finding a girlfriend. 'I don't have anyone at the moment,' he said. 'But what I really want now is to get loved up. Apparently it's fantastic when you're in love and I want that. I want to miss someone, y'know? I'm mad for getting loved up.'

And loved up he got, almost immediately. The two fell head over heels for one another and seemed the perfect match: both came from single-sex pop bands; both had a wild streak; and both were young, good looking, rich and successful. How could they not get on? 'He's brilliant fun,' said Nicky of her new amour. 'We have such a good laugh together when we see each other. We just clicked. He's the sort of guy I've always been looking for. We haven't actually been seeing one another all that long. But I've got to admit that, when we are away, I do spend a lot of time on my mobile phone to Robbie.'

Robbie was on a roll. He and Nicole were openly affectionate with one another at the Brit Awards in February – the same awards show at which Robbie teamed up with Tom Jones to belt out a raunchy duet.

Nicole was beside herself with pride for her new man. 'He was absolutely amazing and I was so proud of him,' she said of his performance. 'He has worked really hard and has so much pressure to deal with. But he is in brilliant form. He is just fantastic. Robbie is always going to be in the public eye because he was in Take That and that does put pressure on any relationship. He is one of the sweetest people I have ever met and I can't imagine how he has managed to cope with all that attention.

'He has a reputation for being wild but that is not the Robbie I know. We didn't want everyone to know about us at first because it makes things so difficult. It's hard for us to be together because we are both so busy all the time and we don't get to see as much of each other as we'd like. But Robbie is so much fun. He really makes me laugh and I hope we last a long time. Though we are both too young to be committed yet.'

Tom Jones was also impressed with his new friend. 'That boy has so much energy he makes me feel young again,' he said. 'In fact, he made everyone in the room feel younger. I think he is one of the most talented and natural performers in Britain today.'

Nicole's band All Saints won an award for best single and best video for 'Never Ever'. Robbie watched Nicole collect the trophies with all the pride of a besotted boyfriend. 'It was so sweet,' he said. 'I just wanted to give her a big hug.'

The relationship quickly became serious, with Robbie talking about the possibility of the two of them having children. 'I want a kid!' he said. 'Last year I found myself getting really broody – it was a major thing for me. I've deliberately tried to calm myself down because eventually I want to be a good role model to my kids. I've been there, seen it and done it, and if my kids want to have a go at it, then fine, I'll be able to talk to them about it. I've even written a song called "If I Ever Have A Son".'

He'd written another song, too, 'Let Me Entertain You', his sixth solo single. It was released in March 1998 and reached Number 3 in the charts. 'Things are phenomenal at the moment, but it's no surprise,' said Robbie smugly. 'I wouldn't have started out in music if I didn't think I could be the biggest in the world. It's all there for me as long as I stay tip top.'

He was staying tip top, even risking the odd drink again, although in great moderation. Asked if he'd been back to rehab, he replied, 'Not true. One minute I'm going for a quiet pint, the next thing they've got me in rehab. It's water off a duck's back just as long as me and my family know what's true. I know I fucked up big time. But the great thing about the British public is that they know that and they'll forgive you if you're good. Staying away from drink was a day-to-day struggle for a long time. I'd think about it all the time, every day, without fail. In the last couple of weeks my life has suddenly become a joy again, and now I think about my music instead of drink. If I want a beer, I have one. I just don't feel like one often.'

The reason for this sudden happiness was clear: Nicole. 'She's the one,' said Robbie. 'We're getting on very well together and we're happy. I can't explain why we get along so well but it has a lot to do with the respect we have for each other. Obviously it's tricky because I miss her when we're apart and she misses me. You've got to accept that we're two young, very successful people and I'm glad that we both have our own lives to lead. If we are to stand the test of time then we'll just have to accept the circumstances. But I definitely see this as a long-term relationship.'

Indeed he did: in June that year, he proposed to Nicole. She accepted. 'Yes, we are engaged. I'm extremely happy,' said an ecstatic Nicole, brandishing a huge emerald engagement ring. It emerged that Robbie had got down on one knee just before a major solo concert at the Royal Albert Hall and asked Nicole to make an honest man of him.

'I was absolutely thrilled,' she said. 'I didn't know quite how to react except to say yes. I have to say his proposal did come as a surprise – but a very pleasant one. I'm over the moon about it and couldn't be happier. The ring he bought me is beautiful and very special and we had a bit of a celebration of our own afterwards.' The couple's schedules, however, meant that a date could not yet be fixed. 'We are both very busy at the moment,' Nicole continued. 'I'm away a lot with All Saints and Robbie is touring, so who knows when we will get the chance to tie the knot?'

Jan Williams was delighted. 'I am very proud of Robbie and his choice. She's a lovely lady,' she said. 'I am very pleased for them both. I have met Nicole quite a few times and I was aware the engagement was coming up. They are both lovely people and are just so in love and so happy. The world is their oyster. I have met her family and they are lovely, too. No date has been arranged, they both have a lot to do with their careers yet.'

And Robbie's career was going from strength to strength. 'I look at Robbie today and I'm so pleased for him because he's done it,' Kevin Kinsella said at the time. 'I knew he had it in him to do it, but I also knew he had it in him to destroy himself because that's just Robbie. People may think he has a great life because he's young, rich and famous, but that boy is driven by demons that have haunted him ever since he first got involved with Take That, when he was 15.

'The day he left the band, he sat down with his mum, Jan, and me at her house and cried like a baby. He was totally messed up. He was pretty much off the rails at that point. He may say and others may say that he went wild because he'd been let off the leash from being in a teen band, but I believe he was just trying to blot out the things that happened to him over the past five years.

'Robbie is basically a lovely, affectionate loveable kid, but he's very easily led and very easily influenced. The drink and drugs did a lot of damage and it's ironic that, in many ways, the whole period which was so bad for him mentally was actually good for his career, because it made him interesting, exciting and credible. He did it at the right time and he was always in the right place with the right people. People used to take bets on how long it would take for him to blow his brains out on drugs. It was really sad. I knew he wouldn't, because he's driven by a terror of failure, a terror of being forgotten.

'I once arranged for him to go on the pitch at Port Vale and he was booed and had things thrown at him. I've never seen someone fall apart like he did then. He made me drive him miles away from the place. He was broken apart. Robbie just wants to prove he is somebody special, but he wants it so much he sometimes goes over the top and that's when the problems start. I just hope he hangs on to it this time.'

Robbie's father, Pete, by now working as head entertainer at Alvaston Hall Hotel in Nantwich, Cheshire, was equally pleased for his son. 'When Robbie was 14, he came to me and said he wanted to get into showbusiness and I gave him one piece of advice: "Don't do it",' he recalled. 'I have to admit now that I was wrong. He's done really well for himself and I'm proud of him. He's a very clever lad.' He also finally got his much-longed-for first solo Number 1: with the hit single 'Millennium'.

When Nicole and her sister Natalie published their autobiography *Forever* some years later, Nicole told about her relationship with the star. The couple's first proper meeting was at the rehearsals for December's Concert of Hope for the Diana, Princess of Wales Memorial fund and Nicole invited Robbie to her birthday party the night before the concert, she wrote. She describes her nerves at the strength of her attraction to Robbie and how she was overwhelmed with strong feelings when they posed for a picture together. They only briefly spoke to each other after the next day's performance but Nicole decided to get Robbie's phone number from her manager.

Nicole described their first date: dinner at the countryside studio where Robbie was working on his album. They ended up getting so drunk at a nearby pub that they passed out on the sofa and Nicole had to leave early the next morning to make it to a video shoot. A week later, a worse-for-wear Robbie called Nicole, desperately asking her to pick him up from a party, and she stayed at his flat and nursed him through the night. They managed to keep the beginning of their affair secret for a few more days until Nicole was pictured leaving Robbie's flat two days after the New Year.

The couple were soon deeply in love and spent every spare moment together. After just three months, Nicole found out she was pregnant at the same time as bandmate Melanie Blatt. Both girls were ecstatic and Robbie shared his girlfriend's happiness. Unfortunately, the rest of All Saints were not as pleased and neither were their record company. Robbie, who was in the process of buying a flat, took Nicole to view it, and pointed out which room he had already earmarked as the nursery. The couple decided to call their child Grace if it was a girl and Robbie wrote a song for his unborn baby, which appears on his *I've Been Expecting You* album.

While All Saints were in New York for a week, the pressure on Nicole reached new levels and she was called in to see record bosses who had made arrangements for an abortion should she decide not to have a child. Completely worn down, Nicole wrote that she decided she had no other option and phoned Robbie with the news, who straight away flew out to America by Concorde to offer his support.

After the operation, Robbie tried his best to comfort his distraught girlfriend but the episode marked the beginning of the end, according to the book. They stayed together for several months but they were beginning to drift apart, prompting Robbie to call Nicole while she was with All Saints in Rio and break off their engagement, blaming work pressures. When Nicole returned home, Robbie had changed his mind and they got back together saying they missed each other too much to stay apart.

Nicole described the beginning of the end. The pair split up and got back together one more time before that Christmas. Nicole had joined Robbie in Amsterdam, where he left 1,000 red roses in her hotel room. Back in England they made plans to have Christmas dinner with Nicole's mother, but the day was ruined when Nicole had to cover up for Robbie who had been so drunk the night before that he couldn't manage to eat anything, she wrote. He got drunk again after lunch and left after arguing with Nicole. The next day's papers were full of pictures of

Robbie unconscious in a hotel lobby covered in shaving foam and toothpaste. When Nicole went to his flat to collect her things, Robbie was still drinking and she told him it was over for good.

At the time, the split was blamed on Nicole's partying. 'Robbie's gone and called off the romance with Nicky and this time we all reckon it's for good,' said a friend. 'He's kept quiet about the whole thing since he had the row with Nicky late last week. Basically, I don't think Robbie thought she was ready to settle down properly yet. Nicky's still bang into the whole pop-star-lifestyle thing. She loves the booze, parties, clothes, good times and all that. I just think Robbie couldn't handle it any more, especially because of what he's been through in the past.'

Nicole was discreet. 'The engagement is off,' she said at the time. 'Robbie and I are no longer an item. Things just haven't worked out. We are still trying to stay friends and talk a lot on the phone. I don't bear him any bad feelings and I know we will always be close. But at the moment, we just can't be together.'

In fact, Robbie was devastated. 'I'm totally gutted,' he said as he was pictured on the verge of tears. 'Nicole means the world to me. I hope we can sort things out.'

Jan was also concerned that the split would push Robbie over the edge again. 'It was a match made in heaven,' she said. 'If they do not make up, he could sink into a real depression. I do not think Robbie could have made a better choice than Nicole. This is all very sad.'

Utterly miserable, Robbie jetted off to Marbella with a group of friends to try to forget his woes. 'I'm the loneliest man in the world,' he said. 'It's been a really hard time. I'm lonely and I'm lost. Sure, I've got a lot but I'm only human. I'm hurting right now. I'm just trying to take it all in and understand what's gone on.'

They got back together briefly, only to part again. Poor Robbie. Even when he was utterly and sincerely heartbroken, he couldn't stop himself from spilling out his sorrows to all and sundry and he has never, from that day to this, become as close to another girlfriend as he was to Nicole.

And so Robbie drowned his sorrows in his own inimitable style: he embarked on yet another bender, was linked to yet more women, worried his mother and ended up on his own. Nicole was to end up with Robbie's arch rival, with whom she now has a child. She and Robbie have not, by any stretch of the imagination, remained close.

8

WILLIAM THE CONQUEROR

Robbie's engagement to Nicole might have hit the buffers, but his career was soaring along as never before. It was quite simple: the audiences loved Robbie and Robbie loved the audiences. He might have found it difficult to maintain a one-on-one relationship, but put him in a building with a few thousand screaming fans and everyone was happy. In 1998, Prince Charles asked him what he had had to cancel in order to attend the Prince's birthday bash at the Lyceum: nothing, said Robbie, apart from world domination.

And the key to it all was his vulnerability. Robbie might by now have become the rock star he longed to be in the days of Take That, but beneath it all was the little boy who wore his heart on his sleeve and could get as carried away by excess as a child in a sweet shop. Another Robbie fantasy is to be James Bond – hence the 'Millennium' video, in which he lifted a quizzical eyebrow, à la Sean, Roger and co. – but whereas Bond is the acme of sophistication, Robbie is the eternal child. He might have been sleeping with groupies and snorting cocaine – but still he comes across as cheeky little Robbie, always wanting to be the centre of attention. It was, in some ways, the same performance that he had been putting on since he was four years old.

Nowhere was this more evident than in his stage performances. At the beginning of 1999, Robbie was engaged on a sell-out solo tour and each concert kicked off with typical self-deprecating humour: a montage of newspaper clippings including 'How drink and drugs ...' and 'Who ate all the pies'. Once onstage, Robbie continued the charm offensive. A typical opener would go thus: 'What a fantastic night I had last night. Somehow I believe it's going to be even better tonight!' Cue screams.

Later on in the show, Robbie would talk about his heartache over Nicole – 'So I went to Benidorm with the lads but deep down inside I didn't want to be in bed with some trollop, I wanted to be with somebody who loved me' – before moving in for the kill. He asks the crowd to blow on him 'so I can feel you' before announcing, 'I love you all, and I don't mean that in a Celine Dion way or a Michael Jackson way. I genuinely love you all.' The feeling was clearly mutual. How could anyone resist this?

The golden touch extended elsewhere. On Christmas

Day 1998, Robbie's father, Pete Conway, joined his son on stage for a duet, when they sang a Frank Sinatra number, 'That's Life'. Pete promptly garnered a fan base of his own, with girls weeping and screaming wherever he went and a massively increased demand for appearances. He was astounded. 'Everything's started to happen for me again since that duet,' he said. 'It is quite unbelievable how much attention is coming my way. I've been asked to perform on television and the crowd sizes have really gone up at my shows.

'I've been Pete Conway, entertainer, for 32 years and now suddenly I am Rob's dad – that's my new role in the entertainment business. I am finding it very interesting. People react to me differently when they know I am his father. Some girls who come to my shows have even cried. I've never experienced anything like it.'

Robbie was, quite literally, on a winning streak. Attending the races at Haydock Park, he practically went through the entire card – and gave a helping hand to others along the way. 'He told us he had picked four winners,' explained a companion. 'What's more, he told the people in the executive box which horses he was going to back. They followed his advice and duly presented him with a bottle of champagne. Robbie was dead chuffed.'

It came as no surprise in February when Robbie was nominated for a record-breaking six Brit Awards. 'Robbie totally dominates this year's shortlist,' said a

Brits spokesperson. 'He has clocked up the highest number of nominations ever. The man is simply irrepressible. Robbie stole the show last year duetting with Tom Jones – and there was real chemistry between them. And Robbie hasn't been out of the charts since.' He was given star billing, supported by Boyzone, Placebo and David Bowie, the Manic Street Preachers, Cher, Whitney Houston and the Eurythmics. And then, perhaps not surprisingly, given his penchant for disrobing in public, Robbie was voted as the man most women in Britain wanted to see strip. (Prime Minister Tony Blair only made number 9 on the list.)

It was at around this time that Robbie started to collect the many tattoos that now festoon his body. His interest was sparked during a visit to Amsterdam's Tattoo Museum, where he heard a talk by the Maori artist Te Rangitu Netana, one of New Zealand's best-known tribal artists. Robbie decided to have one himself on the spot. 'The tattoo Robbie has is basically the story of his life, but using Maori myth and symbolism,' said Te Rangitu. 'It is about self-respect and empowerment and is entirely personal to Robbie. We discussed what is involved in traditional tattooing and I did it later the same day. We started around noon and finished late at night. It's not like normal western tattooing, it's much more of a ritual.'

The tattoo, which extends from Robbie's right shoulder almost down to his elbow, is nothing like a conventional tattoo. Unlike western designs, which are normally chosen from a book of images, the tattoo first involved a long conversation analysing the subject's personality, which meant that Te Rangitu, who had been trained by his father and grandfather, had to learn much about Robbie before he could begin.

'He was a bit nervous when he came in, but he soon relaxed and we sat down and started joking,' said Te Rangitu. 'Because the tattoos are a representation of the other person, I needed to get to know him. I told Robbie about our legends and culture, and he began talking about his own belief system. His tattoo is a symbol of self-empowerment, based on a shark and the sea, images adapted to his own life. The sea represents speed of thought or swiftness of mind. I took into account his beliefs and what he told me about his family, his ambitions and his childhood.'

The design also incorporated representations of the forest, war and peace, which in Maori culture are linked to aspects of the personality. 'The underlying message is that, if you respect yourself, then that's the starting point for respecting everything else,' said Te Rangitu. 'It's a good thing that he is wearing it. Even so – it still hurts. Robbie's tattoo took about three hours and towards the end he was getting pretty sore.'

Robbie's own attitude to the tattoo was a little puzzling. 'I'm having it done because I don't like myself very much,' he said. 'I think it's gorgeous and it's a prayer, protecting myself from me.'

He might have been feeling some regret. The

relationship with Nicole now well and truly over, Robbie took time out for a trip to the United States, where 'Millennium' was to be released. 'We're not going out with each other any more,' he told a US magazine. 'It's one of those things. When you're 25, commitment's a miracle. I'm as fickle as anyone my age, I think. People want security from me and I'm not of a right mind to give it at the minute, especially in the world I live in. I've got the devil in me. I don't know if it's abnormal or if it's just what 25-year-olds feel, but I can't trust myself. Substance abuse. Drinking. Sex. Or throwing myself off balconies, you know, just normal stuff.'

Otherwise, though, Robbie was enjoying the unusual sensation of anonymity. No one in the States remembered him from Take That (if, indeed, anyone remembered Take That) and Robbie, far from worrying that he had not yet broken that notoriously difficult market, relished moving around without anyone realising who was in their midst. 'I've had the best time since I've been famous in the last seven days – nobody knows who I am,' he said. 'It's been really relaxing and, apart from the fact that I want to get laid – that's pretty difficult because no one knows who I am – I've really, really enjoyed having that anonymity.'

Robbie went on to joke about the upcoming awards. 'I've been nominated for six Brits, I don't know what they are,' he said. 'I think it's everything to do with male. I'm thinking of having a sex change. I keep winning everything male – it's getting boring now. So what I'm gonna do is have the snip.' He also talked about the possibility of a film and a book. 'Because I've performed in front of so many people, it gives me the confidence to try anything,' he said. 'I'm white knuckling it all the way. I just feel the fear and throw myself at it.'

Back in the UK, Robbie continued to win plaudits with ease. The *Observer* called him 'the new Elton John'. The *Independent* cited him as a 'laddish Lazarus'. The *Express* asked, 'Can Robbie Take Over The World?' It was heady stuff for anyone, especially with the Brits looming up ahead. Robbie viewed them with a certain foreboding.

'I like awards, I just don't like the ceremonies,' he said. 'They're full of people pretending to be more famous than the other people there. I get claustrophobic at those things, apart from when I'm on stage. But don't get me wrong, I like receiving the awards. I want recognition that I'm here and that I've made an impression. It's like being an ice-cream maker and being told by your distributors that they want to give you an award for the best ice cream. They're putting my albums out, they're making me what I am and it's important that I'm there. There are a lot of things I disagree about within the music industry but, at the end of the day, I'm in that industry.' He was also concerned about what he would win. 'I haven't won anything really big for music,' he said. 'I mean, it's nice winning Best Male and stuff, but that's because they like your personality. I want something for writing a song that's good. That would mean a lot to me.'

Robbie also recognised quite how far he had come since his 2-year-long 'lost weekend'. People were taking him seriously as an artist now, not just an ex-boy band member who couldn't cope with life on the outside. 'The doors have really opened up, so I can do things that are really interesting,' he enthused. 'Last year, people wouldn't have me on their show, wouldn't have me in their magazines, or in their films, but they want me now and that's great.

'I've dealt with so much bad press in the past, I'm not that comfortable having good press. I've been terrified for the last month, but I've come to the conclusion that whatever happens will. But it is quite an undertaking. I just stick my entertainment face on and do it.' But, yet again, doubts were surfacing as to what he really wanted from life: 'That's what getting up on stage feels like to me,' he went on, 'major karaoke on a grand scale. I mean, I'm not a proper musician. It's just a great hobby. I'm an actor who sings songs.' That was quite some statement for a man who had by this time sold over three million albums and whose song 'Angels' had been played 41,931 times on the radio in 1998, making it the most played track of the year. It also earned him £500,000 in playback fees alone.

Certainly, just about everyone else thought of Robbie as a musician. As the Brit Awards neared, bookies were offering just 2–1 for Robbie to take four awards. Fans were betting heavily. 'He's the man of the moment and punters have steamed in to back him,' said Graham Sharpe of William Hill. 'That's why he's been given such prohibitively short odds.'

Robbie made a spectacular entrance into the Brits: he shot down towards the stage on a 50-foot-high wire, a stunt that almost ended in tragedy when he gashed his head on a wooden gantry during rehearsals. 'He really took a bashing and we thought our worst nightmare had happened,' said one horrified onlooker. 'Mercifully, he is made of sterner stuff.' Robbie was able to stage his entrance as planned, an entrance that he then followed up with a spectacular performance. He might have had nerves about the evening, but he pulled it off in true superstar style.

In the event, Robbie won three of the most prestigious Brit Awards – Best British Male Solo Artist, Best British Single with 'Angels' and Best British Video for 'Millennium'. 'I feel really happy and I know my mum will be really proud of me,' he said as he collected the awards. 'I would not be anywhere without her. I've made a lot of mistakes. So many I can't remember half of them. My mum always believed in me and thankfully, so did a few others. I sorted myself out and got back to doing what I wanted to do, which is to entertain people.'

Fatboy Slim, when accepting an award for Best British Dance Track, held up a card with 'Speechless' written on it; Robbie responded, when his second award was announced, by holding up a card bearing the word 'Legless'. The audience loved it.

Robbie himself was thrilled. He had finally been acknowledged by his chosen profession and no amount of clowning around could disguise that. 'I've got three little ladies in my life, now – my Brits,' he crowed. 'How many more do I need? These three awards mean more to me than anyone will ever know. For three years I've been going to sleep at night dreaming about what I was going to say, but when it actually happened I was speechless, which is pretty unusual for me.' He and his mother then celebrated – by going back to Robbie's flat for beans on toast.

'It was an absolutely fantastic night for Robert,' Jan said later. 'I had a gut feeling he would do extremely well and was not surprised when he won three awards. The whole family are very, very happy. I haven't done anything any mother wouldn't do. His success is totally down to his own hard work and commitment to be the best.'

Jan's relief that her son had overcome at least some of his demons was palpable. 'They were bad, they were bad,' she said of Robbie's wild days in a television interview later that week. 'I am really glad they are behind us. As a mum, whenever your children are hurting and suffering, it is as sad for the parents as it is for the child, no matter what age. I found it really, really hard to cope and I know Robbie did. He grieved for my hurt too and so we sort of got through it together. What we found with Robert was that he was ill – and it is an illness when you have a problem with alcohol and drugs. We're talking about 30 and 40 per cent of youngsters and adults who have a problem. When you actually have that illness, it is hard enough to deal with it in private.

'As a mum, I found it really, really hard when I opened a newspaper in the morning or someone would post something through my door with a photograph of him in the paper. But I will say in all fairness to Robert, he shared such a lot with me that it helped me very clearly to understand what was happening to him. Whatever we do in our own lives, we take responsibility for it. I think Robbie underestimated his ability to succeed on his own. He is a very strong young man. Yes, I have been supportive, but everything he has done has been down to him.'

Having had to live through Robbie's dark days, his mother's delight in her son found constant expression. 'Robert's a good role model,' said a proud Jan, when asked about the secret of his success. 'He's honest, hard working, loving and kind. I think he appeals to so many people because they sense he is like them. He's just a well-mannered, down-to-earth young man, who has this ability to communicate with young and old.'

Players in the music industry agreed. 'There's an irony in his lyrics that people identify with and, whether he's singing, dancing, presenting or chatting to

Parky, he has a wit and confidence about him that never fails to amaze,' said Katie Conroy, who handled his publicity at Chrysalis, before adding that he was going to be one of the greatest entertainers of his generation.

But the complexities of Robbie's personality were never far from the surface. Far from being off the sauce, he lurched from sobriety to drunkenness to sobriety again as he struggled to come to terms both with his addiction and his fame. One journalist who saw him on a bender was so alarmed by his behaviour that he actually rang the record company. 'I told them, "I was around Jimi Hendrix before he died and I was around Brian Jones before he died and, if you don't sort this out, he'll be with them by the end of the year,"' he said.

In the event, mercifully, he was wrong, but he was not alone in his concerns. Ray Heffernan, a songwriter who had worked with Robbie in the past, also spoke out to warn his old friend. 'He has what he always wanted but most feared – he has the stardom and he has become "The Man",' he said. 'But it's very dangerous for him because it goes to his head. He tends to drink on it and he puts everything at risk when he does that. He craves success and acceptance, but he has a problem dealing with them.'

Indeed, Robbie was also beginning to show another worrying trait, one that has been growing to this day and might eventually bring him down: arrogance. In classical literature there is the idea of the tragic hero: a great man who nonetheless has a tragic flaw that finally destroys him, such as Othello, who let his jealousy bring him down. With Robbie, if he doesn't learn how to control it, it may well be his arrogance. The great British public can forgive his vulnerability – indeed, they relish it – and his weakness for drink and drugs, but arrogance is another matter.

This was clearly on display when he went to receive an award for Best Male Artist at the MTV Europe Awards. He snatched the trophy out of the hands of a bemused George Michael, with the words, 'Damn right.' He followed that up with a VH1 special in which he confessed that, yes, he did think he was rather wonderful. It was not the kind of performance that endeared him to his fans.

But for now, at least, his behaviour was not totally out of control. His sense of humour was certainly intact: it emerged that he had appeared, heavily disguised, as an extra in *EastEnders* and *Only Fools and Horses*, with a clue to his appearance in the latter signalled by the jukebox playing 'Could It Be Magic' by Take That. 'He pops up whenever he can sneak on to a set,' said a friend. 'It's a hobby. He isn't interested in speaking parts and just gets a buzz out of having his face on his favourite shows. But he doesn't claim the £60 he's entitled to.'

Nor was his popularity waning with the fans. A 21-date concert tour called 'One For The Rogue', taking in 13 cities, was announced: tickets sold out in four hours. He also continued to lavish gifts on his mother as a way of thanking her for helping him through his problems: this time, he bought a £20,000 Andy Warhol print of Grace Kelly from, of all people, Lord Archer. 'This is the second picture he has bought,' said a beaming Archer. 'I put my collection up for sale because I've done my pop art period. Robbie might be a pop star with a reputation for wild ways, but I found him very charming and well mannered. It's so charming that Robbie's bought this picture for his mother. I know she'll really love it. While he was choosing, he got his mother on the phone as we went through the various pictures and she opted for the pink Grace Kelly.'

The clowning around continued. Robbie went to Ireland for three sell-out shows and nearly got into trouble with the management when he was spotted playing football with a group of workmen in the afternoon before the concert took place. 'I had no idea it was Robbie at first,' said MCD concert promoter Jason Green. 'I just saw this young guy with a shaved head in a boiler suit playing football, when I thought Robbie was supposed to be rehearsing. It was only when I shouted at him to stop messing and get out, I copped on who he was.'

Robbie repeated his antics later in the evening: fellow guests at the exclusive Merrion Hotel, where Robbie was staying in the £675-a-night Lord Fitzwilliam suite, complained about him playing football in the corridors of the building.

On another occasion, in Aberdeen, Robbie appeared

outside his hotel dressed in a black Afro-style wig, black bin liner, dark glasses and a Hitler moustache, handing pieces of marzipan with 'RW' scrawled on them to fans, while singing, 'Let it snow, let it snow, let it snow.' The fans were delighted. Rather more worryingly, it emerged that Robbie was checking into hotels as 'God Himself'. The battle with his ego was clearly under way.

The battle with the rest of the world still appeared to be raging, too. At the selfsame Brit Awards where he had been so heralded, Robbie had been deeply upset by the appearance of Nicole in a very revealing outfit, escorted by another pop star, Huey of the Fun Loving Criminals. His weight, always an indicator of his inner turmoil, began to creep up again and he gave an appearance at Wembley punctuated by mooning, smoking and swearing. It seemed that yet another downward spiral had begun, but Robbie picked himself up almost immediately and gave a second Wembley performance 24 hours later that bore no resemblance to the first. 'He was articulate, witty and very entertaining,' said an onlooker. 'There was no way he had been drinking. Whatever was bothering him on Friday seemed to have passed.'

But others in the industry were concerned. They had seen Robbie go off the rails before and were worried that it could happen again – and this time there was a lot more riding on it. Unlike the time when he had left Take That, Robbie was now a major star in the middle of a tour, and a great deal of money was at stake if he fell apart again. Clearly the split with Nicole hurt him more than he'd let on – Robbie is a man who can be very hurt by rejection. His reputation as a womaniser, after all, is based on his casual flings not his more serious relationships and, if the world is divided into leavers and leavees, Robbie definitely falls into the latter category. Jacqui and Nicole, Robbie's two most serious girlfriends, were both the ones to leave, and it looked like Robbie was feeling it.

'Robbie is obviously not a happy young man at the moment,' said one music industry insider. 'It's clear he's stuck in one of those hedonistic self-destructive moods which seem to take him over every few months. If he is not careful, he could throw it all away. The Robbie we're seeing now is, unfortunately, far more like the Robbie we saw go off the rails two years ago.'

He certainly had a lot on his mind. The court case with Nigel Martin-Smith was continuing, with Robbie appealing against the £90,000 award he had been ordered to pay his old manager in November 1997. Yet more gory details surrounding Robbie's departure emerged: his barrister, Michael Silverleaf, told the court, 'If Mr Martin-Smith had given Robbie the same sort of care and affection as the other members, he'd still be managing Robbie and everyone would be happy.' As ever, Gary and Jason emerged as the villains of the piece: 'Orange told Williams, "If you are going, go now so we can get on with it,"' Silverleaf said. More allegations flew. The bitterness intensified.

Robbie was not so numb with misery about Nicole that he had forsaken other women altogether: by now, he seemed to have developed an infatuation with Andrea Corr, the beautiful lead singer of the Irish band The Corrs. He sent her several huge bouquets of flowers with a card bearing the message, 'What Can I Do To Make You Love Me' – the title of The Corrs' huge hit single. Andrea was not sure what to make of it all. 'She was stunned when she received the first bouquet, let alone the second,' said a friend. 'But she hasn't responded – she doesn't know what his situation with Nicole is and she knows her, too.' Indeed, Robbie and Nicole were still in contact, enjoying the odd evening out together, although it was never going to amount to anything more than that.

He was beginning to see other girls, though. He had a fling with Jasmine Jeffrey, who was then starring in the musical *Grease* as prim and proper Sandy, the role made famous by Olivia Newton John. Jasmine promptly opened her heart in a lurid kiss and tell – 'his lips explored every part of my body ...'

Robbie responded in typical Robbie style: he completely ignored it and came up with a new line of his own. 'People are sick of seeing somebody taking themselves so bloody seriously,' he said. 'They want to see somebody make an idiot of themselves – and that's me. I tried to wear a dress last year and that didn't work. I don't know what's next really. Donkey sex?'

He was also beginning to collect more tattoos. 'I went

to Sunset Strip [in LA] opposite the Viper Room last night and got a lion tattooed on my arm for protection,' he said. 'I've got a Celtic Cross on my leg and that's protection. I need to be protected because I've got the devil in me.'

The quest for world domination continued. Robbie played dates in the USA and Canada as well as Europe. March saw the release of 'Strong', another hit which peaked at Number 4 in the charts. His mother Jan gave some clue as to how her son managed his life: 'Robert chooses the people who work for him, from the management and band right down to the drivers, security men and tour operators,' she said. 'He picks people who are kind, who he can get on with, as well as being good at their jobs. The band are very close. When they are on tour you often see them playing football together at the back of some arena. It's a way of life, not a nine-to-five job, so the personalities have to be right. As much as Take That was a bit of a horror story at times, it was a huge learning curve.'

The Take That years reared their ugly head yet again when Robbie finally lost his legal battle with Nigel Martin-Smith and was ordered to pay his former manager £1 million. Martin-Smith lost no time in making his own feelings clear. 'Robbie has now had two attempts at trying to persuade a court of law that I acted badly towards him. He has now failed twice,' he said. 'My only hope is that, in time, Robbie will come to see things as they actually were, not as his mother has chosen to see them. On a personal level, I am pleased that Robbie has had continued success after Take That, but I feel that those fans who have only heard Robbie's account of events would be very disillusioned if they heard the whole story. I have great pity for Robbie. I really was very fond of him, but he is not the same lad I took off the dole and made into a star all those years ago.'

Robbie was livid. He failed to appear at the Capital Radio Help A London Child Awards, where he won Best Single for 'Millennium', and was said to have collapsed with a mystery virus, forcing him to call off tour dates. Elton John voiced concern about his young friend. 'I don't know exactly what's going on, but I'm hearing things about him,' he said. 'I just hope he sorts himself and looks after himself. I'm really concerned. He just needs to take it easy. I'm just hoping he's OK.'

Robbie finally called off the rest of his European tour and, with dates in the US looming, caused yet more anxiety in the industry. Officially he was ill but, on the day he should have been playing a gig in Offenbach, he was spotted watching a game of Sunday league football near his home town. 'It may well be that he was feeling a bit better and just needed some fresh air,' said his management hastily.

Robbie finally took matters into his own hands. Presenter Jamie Theakston had just started a new slot on Radio 1: Robbie rang to reassure him on air that he had not gone off the rails again and had only been injured by falling off a quad bike. And indeed, Robbie had no intention of falling off the wagon yet again. He had been in the gutter once too often by this time, even for his liking, and was determined to beat everyone, but everyone, in a full-on assault on the music industry. Robbie's stab at world domination had only just begun.

6

NOTHING EXCEEDS LIKE EXCESS

Robbie was giving an interview. He was talking about his musical strengths and weaknesses. 'I knew I could write poetry,' he said, 'but I also knew that I only knew three chords and these three chords can't last you forever … unless you're Oasis. Meow, put the knife back in the drawer, Mrs Sharp!'

It was war. Robbie was actually giving that interview in the United States, in one of his many attempts to break into that particular market, but it was Britain that was on his mind – especially Britain's then most famous band Oasis. Gone was humble little Robbie from Take That, desperate to hang out with the big boys; in his place was Robbie Williams, now musically in the same league, and keen to show it. It was as if one of the fourth-formers had turned into a sixth-former over night, and neither quite knew how to deal with it. In

January the Gallaghers added fuel to the fire by calling Robbie 'tubby-arsed Williams'. He hit back by announcing that 'I'm nothing like my inbred cousins from Manchester, who spit on the audience.'

Said a friend, 'Robbie used to be quite close to Liam and Noel but there is a real feud developing.' There was indeed, and one that was to intensify. As Oasis's star declined, Robbie's grew. Then there was to be the question of women.

Nonetheless, the management at Robbie's label, EMI, were keen for him to become as famous in the United States as he was in Britain. And there were problems. Robbie's drink and drugs past were not calculated to go down well with middle America, and he was not always reliable, as he had just proved by cancelling the dates on his European tour. So, the music industry was asking itself, could Robbie break the States – or would the States break him?

'He can be a naughty boy but he certainly isn't out of control,' said a senior figure at EMI. 'He is desperate to succeed in the States and we're sure his common sense won't let him go astray on the eve of his big break.' What about those cancelled concerts? 'He certainly was ill, that's not in dispute,' said EMI frostily. 'Then he had to slow down before the States.'

Seasoned industry figures were cautious, though, about his chances. 'They are going to have a lot of image problems with Robbie in the States if they aren't really careful,' said one. 'It's much harder to sell a male solo singer there than anything else. They like their stars very clean cut. The Spice Girls and B*Witched made it because they are clean, simple, pretty and poppy. All Saints bombed because one was an unmarried mother and the others were too old and not girly enough. It's not a sophisticated market. The last solo male star to make it there was George Michael, 10 years ago.'

A sign of what it was going to be like came when Robbie made a brief trip to Canada. Turning up at the ski resort at Banff, Alberta, Robbie went up to the office at Sunshine Village, seeking a free VIP pass and skiing equipment. 'Don't you know who I am?' he asked.

'Actually no,' the three girls on duty replied.

'I'm Robbie Williams,' said Robbie.

'Never heard of you,' said the girls.

There was clearly some way to go.

Back on the other side of the pond, Robbie seemed to be making some headway with Andrea Corr. She had finally replied to his bouquets with a note saying, 'Entertain me.' This Robbie was determined to do and they began to be seen out together, openly kissing and cuddling in public. Spotted having lunch at the members-only Reynard's Club in Dublin, the two appeared to have eyes only for each other. 'Andrea and Robbie were very much a couple and kept kissing,' said an onlooker. 'They didn't seem to have a care in the world and didn't mind who saw them. Robbie was on top form, laughing and joking, and Andrea was really enjoying herself. It was as though he was on stage and putting on a private show for her.'

Backstage, of course, there were the usual complications. Just the night before, Robbie had been with Nicole, to whom he was still clearly deeply attached. Andrea, meanwhile, had been linked both to the Spice Girls' manager Simon Fuller and Bono. But the two continued to be seen together: they were spotted shopping for thousands of pounds' worth of clothes in Brown Thomas on Grafton Street, before dining at Johnny Fox's pub in the Dublin Mountains. Andrea attempted to laugh off the increasing speculation. 'What snog is this you are all talking about?' she joked. 'We were in a big group and everyone was snogging each other.'

And indeed, it was to prove that, once again, Robbie was not going to be lucky in love. He might have been behaving like a besotted teenager, but Andrea was not interested in a serious relationship, as she made quite clear when Robbie, after just two days in Ireland, had to return to London. 'Let's just say it's not as serious as it looks,' said a friend of Andrea's. 'Robbie has finished with Nicole Appleton [sic] and their relationship is definitely off, but there's little chance of romance full time or wedding bells between Robbie and Andrea. As Andrea has been saying, they are only friends. And all the roses and designer labels in the world won't change that.'

Robbie later confessed that she had turned him

down. 'I was hurt when Andrea told me it wasn't working out,' he said to an American magazine. 'I thought, How could you possibly drop me – it's ME from the telly. But she gave me the push all right and I learned a lot from it.'

'Andrea thought Robbie was quite a laugh, but he's just not her type,' said a friend of the singer. 'She didn't want to pursue the relationship and told him quite quickly.'

Nicole Appleton seemed thoroughly fed up with Robbie, as well. Despite the split, she had until now been professing fondness for him, but something finally gave way. 'Robbie's life isn't real,' she snapped. 'He actually leads a pathetic life. Robbie was too unstable for me and I hope he reads that. The constant rowing and his lifestyle drove us apart. I would never have children with him. He is too crazy. The father of my children would have to lead a normal life. I did want a child before the Millennium but now I'm happy to wait a while longer.' This must have been particularly hurtful for Robbie given that he knew – and the public did not – that Nicole had once been pregnant with his child.

As ever with Robbie, he had other worries on his plate, too. One of the most popular songs on his album *I've Been Expecting You* was 'Jesus In A Camper Van', a track that was also due to be included on the forthcoming American-only release *Robbie Greatest Hits*, later *The Ego Has Landed*. It turned out that

Robbie had done some borrowing and was accused of using lyrics from 'I Am The Way (New York Town)' by the legendary singer Loudon Wainwright III. An incandescent Wainwright demanded either that the track be withdrawn from the American album or that he receive royalties of an estimated £4 million.

Meanwhile, Robbie himself was in dispute with a multinational company, after his name had been linked to a smoking campaign run by Benson & Hedges. He had been spotted smoking at the Brit Awards in February and had actually apologised to a fan afterwards, saying he did not want his name to be linked to tobacco. Nonetheless, a teen magazine in Sri Lanka that was heavily sponsored by B&H, called *Golden Tone News*, had printed a photograph of him surrounded by cigarette advertisements. While Robbie was not directly linked to the ads, the message was clear.

'Robbie would never, ever endorse tobacco,' said Julia Lloyd-Price of IE Management. 'He smokes, but he is desperate to give up. He doesn't want to be linked to tobacco. He wouldn't be happy at all for his image to be used in this way.' Indeed not. Quite apart from the fact that the vast majority of smokers hate their habit and wish to give up, it would be commercial suicide for a star of Robbie's stature to endorse smoking – especially with that all-important American market still to crack.

And the bid to take on America continued. Robbie appeared on *The David Letterman Show* in the States to publicise his new album. There he told his genial host that his father was a comedian, but not a very good one, as he wasn't funny. 'But I am,' Robbie went on.

'Your CD is called *The Ego Has Landed*,' replied Letterman. 'Now we know why.'

Unabashed, Robbie went on to talk about what it was like to be a member of Take That. 'It's like getting a job in a shop where you really enjoy being and then realising you have to clean up the dog turd outside.'

This actually went down well with the US audience, perhaps because Letterman is based in New York and the audience there is more sophisticated than its Mid-Western counterpart. Robbie was due to appear at a small-scale gig at the Bowery Ballroom as his US debut: the concert sold out and tickets began to exchange hands at above face value.

There was a lot riding on this and it wasn't just Robbie's career. EMI, Robbie's record company, was not doing well: pre-tax profits were down 26 per cent to £227 million and the company was hoping that Robbie would help revive its fortunes. He even merited a mention in the company's results. 'Robbie Williams is the most interesting thing for us and he's on tour in the US right now,' said chairman Sir Colin Southgate. 'So far, all the signs are good.'

Nothing about Robbie's trip was being left to chance. All too aware of the temptations New York holds for a young and slightly immature man, Robbie was accompanied by none other than his mother and sister, both of whom were determined to keep him on the straight and narrow. 'His mum was worried about what would happen to him in New York,' said a member of his crew. 'The bars open until 4am and buying drugs is as simple as buying groceries. He is under a lot of pressure to be a success here. It's never easy on the road, so, when his mum said she'd join him, we were all delighted. She can get through to him.'

It appeared that Robbie still harboured hopes of getting back together with Nicole. Those words about how messed up he was had hit home and he tried to show her he'd changed. 'He's putting the past and his old habits behind him,' said an insider. 'He's always talking about Nicole and hoping they will sort out their problems. But he knows, if he goes back to his old druggie ways, he's lost her for good.'

Nor was it just Nicole that Robbie was after: he wanted to capture the heart of the States, too. But despite the success of his appearance on Letterman and his concerts, it was not to be: *The Ego Has Landed* went into the Billboard charts at just Number 85. The single 'Millennium' didn't even get into the Top 100. Apart from anything else, the title of the album was not a good idea. Not only is it an absolute myth that Americans lack a sense of irony, but equally, they like to be wooed with a certain amount of tact. A relative unknown turning up on their shores and proclaiming himself the greatest – and from the mother country, at that – was never going to go down well.

Still, everyone involved put on a brave face. 'Robbie is delighted with the chart position,' said a spokeswoman for his record company.

His manager, Tim Clark, was equally chipper. 'He's not known there,' he insisted. 'We're here for the long haul. Robbie is going to make it in America.'

Back in Britain, it was a different matter. Robbie was very much the superstar, which meant that it was not only B&H that sought to associate itself with him. For some months now, a rumour had been circulating that Robbie was to star in a film provisionally entitled *Addict*, said to be a 'grislier version of *Trainspotting*'. At first, Robbie ignored the rumours, but finally, when German publicists for the film sent out press releases suggesting that not only would Robbie star in the vehicle, but that his father would appear, too, he'd had enough.

'We are getting very angry that the publicists keep putting out material saying that Robbie has agreed to act in the film and that he has been offered £1 million,' said a statement put out by IE Management. 'Robbie has never been offered £1 million and he has turned down the role flat. His father has agreed to look at the script, but no more. It is a cheap publicity stunt. Robbie's record company, EMI, has already sent the film people a warning letter. We will have to consider stronger action.' Fame was clearly taking its toll in more ways than one.

But Robbie was gaining increasing recognition as a

musician in his own right – or, at least, teamed with
Guy Chambers. The two were now recognised as one of
the best songwriting teams around, and at the Ivor
Novello Awards, they shared two prizes for 'Angels':
Most Played Song and Songwriter of the Year. Robbie
was clearly thrilled – and defensive. 'I'm going to crack
America,' he said as he collected his awards. 'Some
people had written me off before I'd even got there, but
I will embarrass them. I'm looking forward to doing
really well.

'When I first went solo, I said I wanted to be up there
with George Michael and Oasis and sell as many records
as them. People laughed at me then. But I've got a
message for them – fuck off! I'm in America and I'm
going to make it and you're going to have to eat your
words if you don't believe me. Unaccustomed as I am to
gloating in public, I'll try my best. I am overwhelmed.'

It was understandable that Robbie should want to
crow at those who predicted his solo downfall, but, as
ever, he went too far. That arrogant streak, his fatal flaw,
was making itself felt again and he seemed to realise
this. Backstage, he continued: 'I get a bit dumbfounded
at awards like this. They're a bit overpowering. I'm
often accused of being arrogant but it's just because I'm
scared. I've won something for doing good, for doing a
good thing. I know I can be flippant but this really does
make me very happy.'

As if all this were not enough, on the very same
day, Robbie was voted most gorgeous man on the

planet in the past 100 years, by readers in a poll for *Company* magazine. It was enough to go to any young man's head.

And, despite all the acclaim, Robbie was capable of acts of generosity, especially where his fans were concerned. He played football in a charity tournament at Chelsea's Stamford Bridge ground a couple of days later and was awarded the man-of-the-match cup shortly afterwards. He promptly gave it to Christopher James, a 16-year-old fan of the star who suffered from cerebral palsy. 'Here you go, mate,' said Robbie, ruffling the youngster's hair. 'This is for you.'

It was a lovely gesture and Christopher was obviously moved. 'Robbie's a wonderful man, a great guy,' he enthused. 'I thought he'd played really well and wanted to tell him. I went up, patted him on his shoulder and said, "Well done." Without hesitation, he gave me the trophy, saying, "This is for you." It was absolutely brilliant.'

Robbie's name continued to be bandied about in the gossip columns. He was spotted at Kylie Minogue's 31st birthday party – a friendship that was to bear professional fruit for both in the years to come – and his name was linked to, of all people, Madonna. (This was before anyone knew about Guy Ritchie.) Cynics muttered that, if any meetings had taken place, it was probably a lot more to do with Robbie asking for advice on how to raise his profile in America – and, if so, it worked, to a limited extent at least. Robbie returned to the States to appear at the MTV Movie Awards, where he performed 'Millennium', dressed as James Bond, and thanked the audience with the words, 'Thanks for having me, I'm sure you all will later.' America, a nation divided from Britain by one language, did not get the joke.

But they were beginning to take to Robbie. He performed his first major concert in America at the Mayan Theatre in Los Angeles, where the audience was 2,000 strong. Despite stumbling over some of the words to 'Strong', the hour-long performance went down well, with the usual mix of joking and arrogance. 'You're too kind but very honest,' he told cheering fans. 'It's hilarious but fucking brilliant that someone from a small town in England can have Americans so into his music.' And then came the now usual diatribe against Take That: 'They fired me ... and I went on to sell six million records and tour America,' he roared. 'So fuck them! I'm the greatest release Take That ever had.'

It was all too much for Gary. He had managed to keep his peace time and again, as Robbie gloated over his old band mates but he really could not take it any more. 'It's annoying for me that he is the one who has gone forward and done it,' he said. 'I can't believe it. I can only think he must have a good team around him – like he had in the past. I was with him for seven years and never saw him write a song. It was hard enough for me to get him to sing.' He also admitted the stresses and strains within the group. 'I don't talk to Robbie, we

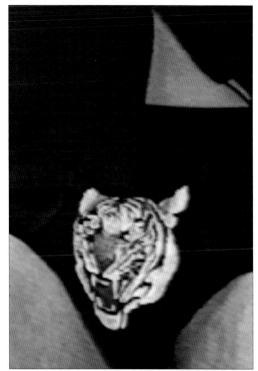

left: Those pants! Robbie proudly drops his trousers on *Top Of The Pops* to show
is favourite tiger underwear.

right: Part of a similar performance!

om: Buy of the Tiger. Robbie models and auctions his pants at Sotheby's for charity.

Bare faced cheek. Robbie pulls one of his famous moons. This one is for the oppositi
after scoring a goal for his favourite team Port Vale in a testimonial game.

Williams cheeky sense of fun is often on display...

: Robbie takes a bath on The Big Breakfast.

om: Robbie bares (nearly) all for Comic Relief in 2003.

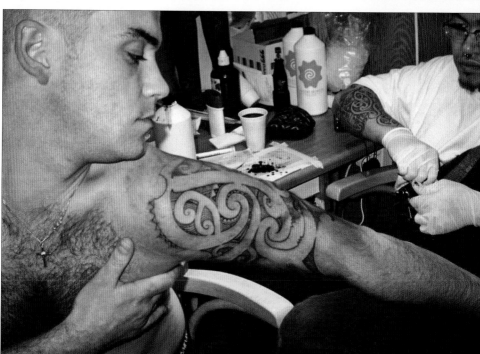

Robbie adds to the many tattoos adorning his body. He sees them as a form of empowerment, with symbolism that gives him self respect and a way of 'protecting myself from me'.

Left: More than just friends? Robbie with close friend Jonathan Wilkes, and (*Top t*) as an irreverent reverend at the first night of *Godspell*, in which Jonathan starred.

om Left: With his song-writing partner, Guy Chambers, before their dramatic split.

om Right: Robbie shops with Elton John, one of his richest fans.

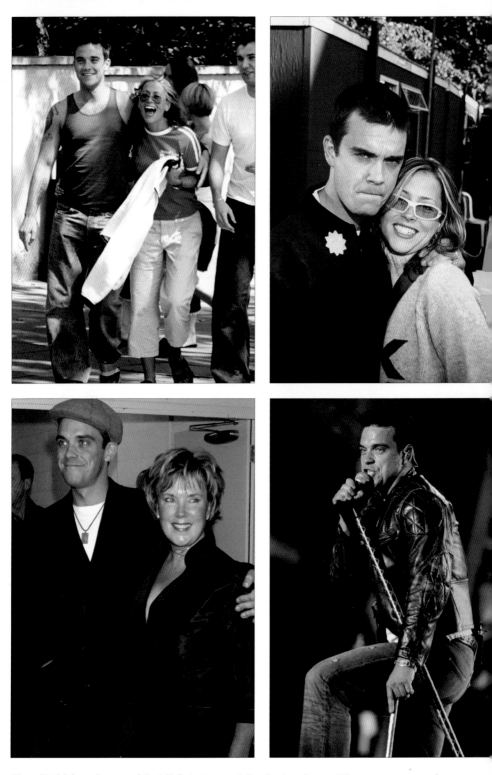

Top: Robbie relaxes with All Saints star Nicole Appleton. They were very close, but ultimately things fell apart.

Bottom: (left) Robbie arrives at the premiere of his film *Nobody Someday* with his mum; (right) on top form at the Tribeca Film Festival in May 2003.

: Over three nights in August 2003, Robbie performed live to over 375,000 people at
bworth, staging the UK's biggest-ever pop concert to date.

om: Robbie followed up his 'Swinging' with a well-received cameo role in the 2004
e Porter biopic *De-Lovely*.

Revelling in being centre-stage in front of the watching world, Robbie stole the show
Live 8 in London's Hyde Park in July 2005.

never have,' he said. 'I don't understand it. He's engineered the whole situation. This so-called row between us is all unprovoked by me. I'm still trying to understand it.' Robbie made no reply.

It was by now the summer of 1999 and, trials and tribulations with the United States apart, Robbie's star continued to burn brightly in the celebrity sky. Ironically, given his performance at school, he was asked to contribute a poem to a new anthology, *Oral*, aiming to make poetry cool. Fellow contributors included Jarvis Cocker and Damien Hurst. 'This anthology is an attempt to reflect the urgency and vitality that abounds in poetry today,' said the book's editor, Sarah-Jane Lovett. 'I wanted to produce a book not for anoraks but a book that is available, up front and open for all.'

Perhaps unsurprisingly, given his feelings towards his old teacher, Robbie's contribution was the lyrics of the song 'Hello Sir', including the line, 'Yes, that's right, my name's Bob, The one who landed the pop star's job.' It was not necessarily the best choice to have made, as the publishers themselves acknowledged – someone found an uncorrected proof copy, upon which was written, 'It is a little turgid, I'm afraid, but it's what his management wants.'

Robbie soon discovered that poetry critics are a good deal harsher than a star-struck fan base. Asked to comment on the work, Al Alvarez, editor of *The Faber Book of Modern European Poetry*, was not impressed. 'This is so foolish and so vulgar,' he said. 'It's directed at an old teacher who tried to keep him in line, and all I can say is that I'm on the teacher's side. If that's what this boy wants, then good luck to him. It's self-aggrandising beyond belief.' There was that tragic flaw making itself felt again … Alvarez was not, incidentally, so harsh on all the contributors. Jarvis Cocker's contribution was judged 'quite promising'.

It was at this point that Robbie's old manager, Nigel Martin-Smith, decided to talk about problems he said were caused by Robbie's mother, Jan. He claimed she was jealous of his relationship with her son. 'It was Robbie's mum who asked me to audition him and, while he was getting to where he wanted, everything was fine,' he revealed. 'But once Mum decided he was a star, the problems started. She resented me taking her place by looking after Robbie. We had band meetings every two weeks and I encouraged them to be honest if they had any problems. Robbie asked if he could bring his mum to the meetings. I refused.'

Martin-Smith was also candid about what was going to be involved in making Take That a success. 'When the boys first got together, I asked them to sign five-year contracts and, if they were successful, they wouldn't want to sign another,' he said. 'After five years of working their socks off, they would hate my guts and probably each other's too. That's exactly what happened. Robbie did have girlfriends on the road – he was the only one who did. I should know – I paid for the champagne breakfasts for them.'

But Robbie's fans took no notice and he was soon winning plaudits again – this time as the Most Kissable Man in Britain. A poll of 17,000 women by the Ann Summers lingerie chain gave Robbie 8,500 votes, with Sean Connery in second place at 3,500, and David Beckham trailing in third, with 3,000. Perhaps unsurprisingly given this, he was then chosen to head up a campaign raising awareness of testicular cancer. The idea was to alert young men to the danger: Robbie cavorted around in a huge pair of falsies before telling men to be aware of their own bodies, too. 'Go check 'em out,' he said, grabbing his crotch. It was a very Robbie way to behave.

And indeed, it seemed that he recognised how fortunate he had been. 'Trite as it sounds, I've had so many opportunities and I wanted to do something good in return,' he said before continuing, 'And it's probably not irrelevant that I've got the biggest left testicle in showbusiness.'

His fortune was growing. By this time, despite his various lawsuits, Robbie was said to be worth about £10 million and he himself recognised quite how canny he'd been in one respect: releasing a song called 'Millennium' just as the world approached that big event. 'I hope it'll provide a nice little nest egg,' said Robbie, acknowledging the ploy. 'Considering I'm not supposed to be that bright, I can't understand why no one did it before me.'

Arrogant, yes – but insecurity lurked beneath the

surface. Asked what got him out of bed in the morning, Robbie replied, 'The need to prove myself wrong. I have to keep rising to new challenges to fight off this voice inside that says I'm not capable of achieving them.' In other words, cracking America. The challenge was still there.

If there were any doubts about Robbie's status back in Britain, these were laid to rest by the news that he was to be included in the millennium edition of *International Who's Who*, joining fellow new additions Catherine Zeta Jones, Des Lynam and Alastair Campbell. 'There's no doubt Robbie is an important star and at the top of the pop world – we are recognising that,' said editor Richard Fitzwilliams.

Robbie celebrated by having a dose of colonic irrigation – 'I literally had the shit taken out of me' – before announcing a new concert in the *Watford Observer* for the 1,800-seater Watford Colosseum. It was not the standard journal of record for a pop concert, but even so, the gig sold out in just two hours. He then played to a slightly bigger crowd a few days later, when he appeared in front of an 80,000-strong audience at Slane Castle in Ireland, alongside the Happy Mondays, Stereophonics, Gomez, Placebo and Cast.

And, as had happened so often before, Robbie went too far. The concert was broadcast live to one million viewers on Sky, with another two million tuning in to hear it on the radio. Unfortunately, Robbie chose the occasion to drop his trousers, clutch his crotch, and let out a string of obscenities, which, he said, he hoped would get him into the *Guinness Book of Records*. Just as with the concert in Manchester in which he'd performed naked, the fans were not impressed. 'He was totally over the top,' said Sarah Driscoll, who attended the concert with her 15-year-old son, Luke. 'Some people here with their children were disgusted. I'd rather Robbie hadn't dropped his trousers, he's talented enough not to do that.' She wasn't the only one who was irate: the Independent Television Commission upheld a complaint against Sky for broadcasting Robbie's behaviour.

The exhibitionism – which was on the increase – might have been a sign of something deeper. All of Robbie's acclaim and success were not proving enough to heal old wounds. Yet again he laid into his old colleagues in Take That and yet again he singled Gary and Nigel Martin-Smith out for particular blame. 'The band had the creativity of mentally unstable morons and was spawned by Satan. The manager Nigel Martin-Smith really mucked me up emotionally,' he said in an interview with a German magazine. 'He managed me and manipulated me from when I was 16. It was a devil's pact – he gave you fame and riches, you gave him your soul and 25 per cent of the takings. OK, I got the riches and fame but I had no respect for what I did. I hated our lead singer Gary Barlow and I hated our music. In the end, I hated myself.

'One song of mine is called "Strong". His [Gary's] last

record was called "Stronger". So I'll have to call my next album *Strongest*. But I shouldn't say anything against Gary. His music makes mine sound like Bach.'

And again he touched on the period after leaving Take That. 'I had taken all possible sorts of drugs and for a long time it was very enjoyable,' he admitted. 'I was called a fat joke and they were right. I was a pitiful, wretched creature. First thing in the morning I would empty a bottle of wine that two hours before I'd fallen asleep over. Then I would take a line of cocaine – otherwise I wouldn't be able to wake up.'

Robbie also talked about the price of fame, now that he had moved into a mansion in London's Notting Hill. 'People ring on the bell and bang on the door and if I press my head against the window for just a couple of seconds there's a crowd outside,' he said, adding, 'I'm single now but maybe my love will be behind the supermarket check-out counter, waiting for me to walk in.'

Love was certainly in the air elsewhere. Robbie sang at the wedding of Guy Chambers, and even did an impromptu caterwaul at the blessing of the marriage between Zoë Ball and Fatboy Slim. More awards rolled in: Robbie was named Solo Artist of the Year at the GQ Men Of The Year Awards. More profitable ventures emerged, as Robbie signed a £2 million deal to promote Pepsi. More good work rolled in, too: Robbie was also one of the performers at NetAid, a giant Wembley show linked to others around the world to help raise money for refugees in Kosovo and the famine in Sudan. It was watched by 50 million people worldwide.

And then it was back, yet again, to the United States for more concerts and more promotion. And yet again, Robbie behaved like an exhibitionist: as 3,000 fans were taking their seats at a concert in Atlanta, Georgia, Robbie wandered out on stage stark naked, his hands alone covering his modesty, before pretending he'd taken a wrong turn and heading back to the dressing room.

It was all beginning to take its toll. Despite the odd descent into drunkenness and bad behaviour, Robbie had been working very hard for two years now and still the United States, bar these smallish concerts, was proving as unreceptive an audience as ever. 'I have got to the point where I'm not arsed about what people think of me and I really have no point in being on stage,' he said in an interview which bore echoes of what he said on leaving Take That. 'I don't know what I want to do but it sure isn't this. It doesn't give me a thrill any more.' He talked about wanting to go into acting, with rumours abounding that Robbie had set his heart on being the après-Brosnan James Bond.

None of it was particularly serious, though. Robbie was clearly utterly fed up with the unreceptive United States, but he was not prepared to throw in his singing career just yet. Britain continued to love him: his November release of 'She's The One' went straight into the charts at Number 1. The year ended on a farcical note, when Robbie was named as the sixth most influential musician of all time – one place ahead of Mozart. Still, no one was taking it too seriously.

He was also named the most popular youth icon of the twentieth century, before cavorting around in a gorilla costume on stage during a performance of the pantomime *Aladdin* at the Brighton Theatre Royal, Sussex. Since he kept the mask on, no one knew it was him. He also announced plans to record another album after all. And so Robbie approached the millennium, jolly, jovial and as messed up as ever. And while you might have thought that someone who had flown so high, on this side of the Atlantic, at least, must be due for a fall, this was not to be the case. In the coming year, Robbie was to scale even greater heights.

10
SING WHEN YOU'RE WINNING

Robbie's winning streak was catching. The latest to benefit was Guy Chambers: Robbie's songwriting partner was becoming a commodity in his own right and was signed up in a £1 million publishing deal by EMI. He was beginning to be noticed elsewhere, too, and had written three new songs for Kylie Minogue's latest album. If Robbie was irritated – and he was certainly to become so – he didn't show it at the time. In fact, he and Kylie were in talks about recording a duet, which was to be released later in the year.

And his wealth was mounting up. Robbie had earned £7.5 million in 1999, £4 million of which he spent on a large three-storey townhouse in Clarendon Road, Notting Hill, an upmarket area of west London. The front door cannot be reached without entry being granted via an intercom, and Robbie's car – with blacked-out windows – sits on the drive, ready for the star to make a quick exit. He had also acquired a flatmate: an aspiring singer called Jonathan Wilkes.

Robbie and Jonathan had known one another all their lives, and it was, in fact, Wilkes who had been performing in *Aladdin* when Robbie made his impromptu appearance. Now he, too, was basking in the Robbie-glow – in his case because he was after a record deal and Robbie co-wrote nine songs for him. Although he was never to acquire anything like the success Robbie has enjoyed, from this moment on he became a permanent fixture in the star's life, living with him when Robbie is in England and looking after the house when Robbie is abroad.

The two were first introduced as children because their mothers were great friends. They struck up a relationship themselves despite a four-year age gap. Jonathan originally wanted to be a footballer and then worked in Blackpool for several years until coming to London, where he and Robbie met up again. 'Rob kindly offered to put me up and that was a godsend, because London can be very daunting and lonely,' said Jonathan. 'I was scared and naïve when I arrived. There were all these famous people coming round to the house and suddenly this whole other world opened up to me. Rob understood that because he's been there himself and he's the best friend I could hope for. He's like a brother.'

The feud with Oasis rumbled on. 'He's a fat dancer

from Take That,' said Noel. 'Somebody who danced for a living. Stick to what you're good at, that's what I always say.'

Robbie responded with a certain degree of style: he sent him a funeral wreath with the message 'To Noel Gallagher, RIP. Heard your latest album – with deepest sympathy, Robbie Williams.'

Robbie also enjoyed a brief romance with television presenter Tania Strecker. But February brought a big upset: he failed to be nominated for the major Brit Award, meriting only the 'Best Video' and 'Best Single' category. The reason was quite simple: to be nominated, Robbie would have had to have released an album in 1999 and he hadn't. Rules were rules and even a singer of Robbie's stature couldn't flout them. Nonetheless, he was livid at the perceived snub and flounced off to New York for a photo session.

The feud with Oasis stepped up a beat. 'We have made the best fucking album out this year – better than anything fatty will ever do,' stormed Robbie's erstwhile friend Liam. 'You can tell the c**t, if I ever see him in a club in London, I'm gonna break his fucking nose. He'll be needing wreaths on his door. Rest in peace!' Robbie appeared pretty relaxed about the threat. 'Oh, he's going to beat me up, is he?' he remarked. 'I'm just not angry enough to hit him – it's not my career going down the drain.'

In the event, Robbie did appear at the Brits and won both categories for which he had been nominated with

'She's The One'. He also used the opportunity to take another dig at Liam. 'Would anyone like to see me fight Liam?' he enquired as he accepted the award. 'Would you pay to come and see it? Liam, a hundred grand of your money and a hundred grand of my money. We can have a fight and we can all watch it on TV. Now what are you going to do?' Back down was the answer, with Liam muttering that it would be 'childish' and 'not what rock 'n' roll is about'.

And these Brits meant that Robbie, by winning a total of nine, had also won a place in musical history by overtaking Annie Lennox, who had won a total of eight. He had rushed back by Concorde for the win, as he explained later. 'I woke up in America this morning and decided to get the first flight back to London because it's the first time I've actually won awards that I think I deserve,' he said. 'I might have been a bit arrogant and drunk before, but this time I am sober and really happy.'

With that it was back to the United States for yet another promotional tour, yet another impromptu strip – this one in the Vietnamese Le Colonial restaurant in Los Angeles – and yet more revelations about his past. The romance with Tania over, Robbie was now claiming to be celibate. 'I'm not planning on becoming a monk, but for the moment I am sleeping by myself,' he told a Californian magazine.

'I need a rest from women. Because of the new regime I'm under, I can now keep my trousers on. In the bad old days, I thought I was supposed to sleep with lots of girls because I was a pop star. That's exactly what I did, because it was handed to me on a plate every single night. In fact, there was too much of it and in the end it didn't make me happy. Unfortunately, the girls I've slept with have a habit of blabbing about it. As soon as they got out of bed, they told the world. My love life is my own business and I am sick of it. I needed to give and receive unconditional love, so I bought two dogs.' This, alas, didn't work either – the pooches made a mess of Robbie's kitchen and so ended up being sent back.

Pausing only to get another tattoo, Robbie returned to London – and bumped into Mark at a celebrity football match. 'I saw him there and said hello,' said Mark, rather wistfully. 'I spoke to him a bit before Christmas but I haven't really had much chance. We're not the best of mates. It's the same with all of them. I see Howard Donald and Gary Barlow now and again, but I haven't seen Jason Orange for quite a while. Apparently he's travelling.'

So was Robbie, and now under the auspices of UNICEF. The singer Ian Dury, a friend of Robbie's, had died at the beginning of the year and UNICEF asked the younger star to step into the shoes of the older. Ian had been a charity ambassador for UNICEF, and now Robbie, who had already been on overseas visits under the UNICEF umbrella, was asked to take on the role of UNICEF UK's special representative to the music industry. It clearly touched him deeply.

'This means so much to me, more than anything else I've achieved in my life, and I thank Ian for introducing me to working with UNICEF,' he said at a dinner thrown by Roger Moore to mark the Act Now 2000 campaign. 'Some of the best moments of my life have been spent with children in Mozambique and Sri Lanka. I am stepping into some very big shoes tonight. Ian is the reason I am here. I am not known for going into anything half-heartedly. I can't take Ian's place – nobody could – but I am going to try my best and just be me. During my last trip I met so many kids who gave me reason to smile. Now I want to be able to give them something to smile about, too.'

Robbie's attachment to Ian was genuine. In June he performed, alongside what seemed to be the entire great and good of the music industry, in a tribute concert to Dury, which raised £50,000 for the charity CancerBacup. He was the last to perform, singing 'Sweet Gene Vincent', before the entire cast joined together in a rendition of 'Sex and Drugs and Rock 'n' Roll'. It was, said one critic, 'an unforgettable sight'.

Along with the great and good, Robbie continued to work on his career – and, as so often happens with Robbie, business and pleasure got mixed up. He had known the diminutive but beautiful Australian pop singer Kylie Minogue since his days in Take That, and talks about the two of them performing together had been ongoing for some time. These talks finally came to fruition when the two recorded 'Kids', which was released later in the year. Asked about it, Robbie responded in typical fashion.

'Well, basically I fancy her,' he said. 'I always have and it's a kick for me. She's a fantastic singer. A lot of personality. Great charisma. I was like, "Kylie, I fancy you. Can you sing on my record, please?" I was really nervous when we got together to sing the duet. I couldn't even speak to her. But I could sing with her. But that's Robbie singing. Robbie can sing with anyone. Robbie's brave.' On another occasion, he was more blunt. 'I asked her if she wanted a really good sex session,' he said.

He was also able to show a very rare flash of humour on the subject of Take That. 'I've been mistaken for Gary Barlow,' he confessed. 'I had a whole conversation with a guy one time and, at the end of it, he said, "Well, it's been a pleasure to meet you, Gary." I just told him it was a pleasure to meet him too.'

Kylie responded with all the grace that is her trademark. 'He's said things like, I make his tummy go funny, and I'm saying "never say never" about so many things right now,' she cooed. 'You never know, it might happen. I think he's well fanciable. First as a pop star, because Robbie is Robbie. But Robbie the person is a cool and complex guy. I think he's very cute.' Kylie was also being tactful. In actual fact, she already had a boyfriend – the model James Gooding, who she had met at the Brit Awards earlier in the year. But she also knew what would make a good story ...

Living up to the rock star image, Robbie bought a £100,000 silver Ferrari with the licence plate number 50 RRY. He then promptly sold it again without so much as taking it for a spin, although he did keep the plate. It seemed there were two problems: first, the minor matter of not having a driving licence; and second, the fact that it was too ostentatious. 'I love having money. I fucking LOVE having money,' he said.

'Where I come from, if you have something nice, invariably people throw things at it. I absolutely hate the idea of having something that's nice and people despising you that much. I bought a silver Ferrari, but then got so embarrassed about this vulgar display of wealth.'

A friend of his thought the first problem might also have preyed on his mind. 'It's not exactly a great image for a rock star – turning up in a flash car with L-plates.'

The readers of *Company* didn't mind: they voted him sexiest man in the world for the second year running. But, as ever, Robbie was going through his own torments, as he talked about his continuing problems with drugs. 'If there was a gram of coke on the table, I'd have to leave the room or else that would be it,' he said. 'It's such an awful drug, I wish they had never invented it. I hate coke. It makes you do anything to get it and you end up in horrible situations with horrible people. It's ugly and undignified and I'd hate to meet me if I was off my head.'

And he was far from being free of its hold. 'I popped

into Soho House for one drink and that was it,' he recalled. 'I don't remember much about it. Didn't take any drugs, though. Not for lack of trying, mind you. I was in the middle of Soho and nobody had drugs.' It also emerged that the sexiest man on the planet was thinking of settling down. 'The difficulty is that the sort of girls who will come home and sleep with me you can't have a conversation with,' he said. 'And I don't just want a conversation, I want a wife and kids. I want a real woman but I keep getting sidetracked.'

That didn't deter the fans even a tiny bit. Robbie's massive popularity was confirmed when he announced a set of tour dates for the autumn – and nearly £7 million worth of tickets were sold in just six hours. There were 20 tour dates, 243,600 available passes and telephone lines opened at 9am: by 3pm everything had been sold. 'The demand we've had in the past for Oasis and even Cliff Richard took some beating,' said a spokesman for Birmingham's NEC, 'but these went like lightning.'

A spokesman for Manchester's MEN Arena was equally taken aback. 'The demand has not surprised us,' he said. 'What has is the speed at which tickets have been snapped up. It has been absolutely spectacular.'

An industry insider summed it up. 'He's the top draw in the world,' he said. 'There's nobody – including Oasis – who can touch him now.'

He did upset some people, though, with the video for his latest single, 'Rock DJ', another Number 1. He actually made two videos to go with the song: one was utterly innocuous (and dull) and showed him messing about in a record studio. The other, however, was rather different. It showed Robbie spinning discs as a string of beautiful women circled around

him, totally ignoring him. To get their attention, he starts to strip (natch) and, when even that doesn't work, he starts pulling off his own flesh and throwing it at the women. They finally turn on him and gorge on his flesh until all that is left is a dancing skeleton. It made quite a contrast from his previous video for 'She's The One', in which he was pictured ice-skating.

The BBC said that there was no way it could show the footage. '*Top Of The Pops* goes out during peak family-viewing time at 7.30pm. And, if we had shown the full video, we were bound to have received complaints. It was just too shocking for us to show to a family audience, no matter how big a star Robbie is. It was unsuitable. The BBC will now show the beginning of Robbie's video tonight, but they will stop airing it before the gruesome finale.'

But, of course, the video had the desired effect: it got talked about. Made by Vaughn Arnell, who was also responsible for George Michael's 'Outside' video, which featured the great man after his arrest in Los Angeles playing an LA cop, the video also featured the likes of Elizabeth Jagger. It was considered another triumph all round.

Robbie could still be prone to extremely erratic

behaviour, however. On his way home from a film premiere, Robbie bumped into his old pal Nick Moran, star of *Lock Stock and Two Smoking Barrels*, and suggested a drink at Soho House. The two then went on to Stringfellows and started ordering champagne. Robbie, as usual, had too much and got carried away: he stripped off and joined the dancers on stage. The bouncers told him to sit back down at which point he had a panic attack, whisked his clothes back on and disappeared – leaving Nick with the £300 bill.

'It was a nightmare,' Nick said afterwards. 'Robbie just suddenly left, having a panic attack, and all the bouncers thought we were doing a runner and collared me. I thought I was in deep trouble and ended up having to pay out £300. I was gutted. I was slaughtered and furious. I rang directory enquiries, going mad, and demanded they find me an R Williams in Notting Hill.' Not surprisingly, Robbie was not in the phone book. But he did hear about his old friend's anger and sent an apology in the form of a bottle of champagne and £300 – in Monopoly money.

Never one to leave his body alone for long, Robbie went out and got a new tattoo reading 'Elvis Grant Me Serenity'. In fact, he was going through something of an Elvis phase at the time: wandering around with a quiff and threatening to open his forthcoming concerts clad in a white jumpsuit. Instead, he fell back on his usual tricks and dropped his trousers at the beginning of a television interview in New Zealand, although at least he had his underpants on. He also talked more about his duet with Kylie.

'She phoned me up and asked me to write and sing a song with her,' he said. 'I thought I was in with a chance of sleeping with her over the course of the next few months that we spent together. I didn't sleep with her and I was seriously thinking of dumping the song from the album because she wouldn't. Kylie's a bit frightening and is a powerhouse of sexuality and deviance.'

Robbie was out to do more than shock, though. After the Stringfellows incident, he had stayed off the booze and was clearly aching to get back on it. 'I am currently on two weeks without a drink,' he admitted. 'And I'm heading somewhere over the next few days to go and do something publicly very bad. So stay tuned.' And what of Robbie's poor, long-suffering mother, Jan? 'Yeah, I think she's scared,' said Robbie.

The next stop was Australia. In the event, Robbie's behaviour was as might be expected: the usual dropping of his trousers in front of assembled journalists to reveal his tiger decorated Y-fronts, another declaration of lust for Kylie and an unsavoury episode in which he urinated in the doorway of a nightclub. But what was really on Robbie's mind was Nicole Appleton. News had just filtered out that she had a new boyfriend: none other than Robbie's bitter rival, Liam Gallagher. Robbie couldn't believe it.

'Robbie thinks her romance with the man he regards as his arch enemy is the ultimate betrayal,' said a friend of Nicole's. 'But Nicole and Liam have always got on well and now they're both single there's no reason for them not to get together.'

Who knows if this had any bearing on Robbie's next move? The timing, however, was certainly interesting. As it was August, Robbie decided he needed a summer holiday – and he did it as publicly as possible. He jetted off to St Tropez.

If Robbie wanted to get the attention of the world's press, he succeeded. He took as his travelling partner one Geri Halliwell, who was in the middle of her transformation from voluptuous Ginger Spice into a pencil, and who had brought with her a succession of increasingly minute bikinis to parade on the beach. Together, Robbie and Geri rented a villa and sat back (or rather, strutted around), waiting for speculation as to the real cause of their holiday. Were they a couple? Were they just friends? Were they, as the two people who had been the first to leave a five-piece manufactured band, just swapping tales of their past? Or were they, heaven forbid, just doing it to get a lot of publicity?

They certainly weren't trying to keep a low profile. Geri gave almost daily displays of yoga on the beach, while Robbie sat around showing off his tattoos. Together they jet-skied around the Mediterranean, before having a public row in one restaurant and another public display of togetherness the next day. Both laughed happily when questioned about the true nature of their relationship and both remained tight-lipped, which served only to fuel the speculation still further. The other Spice Girls publicly warned Geri to be careful: they had, after all, witnessed Robbie's treatment of Mel C, aka Sporty Spice, at close hand. Still no one seemed to realise there was anything coincidental about the timing of two pop stars linking up in the south of France, just as another two pop stars had back in England.

It was one of Robbie's conquests, Vineeta Whyte, who shed true light upon the matter, when she gave a kiss and tell to a Sunday newspaper. After the usual lurid descriptions of what they'd got up to – 'He was without doubt the best lover I've ever had. It was the most torrid sex of my life. I felt waves of excitement running through my body from the first moment he ran his hands up and down me' – she gave a very telling impression of Robbie's state of mind.

'He asked me a bit about myself. But mostly he wanted to talk about Nicole Appleton,' she said. 'It was obvious she's the one girl he can't get out of his head. He asked me if I knew what it was like to feel really close to somebody. He claimed that even after he split up from Nicole she was still the closest person in his life apart from his mum. Robbie went on for a few minutes about how sex with Nicole was different from any other girl. He kept saying things like, "I feel at one with Nicole" and "Me and Nicole clicked".'

Poor Robbie. It must have been dreadful for him to

see Nicole so publicly happy with the man he had grown to loathe – but, if he couldn't have the girl, at least he got the consolation of blanket media coverage. He and Geri continued to hog the limelight: Robbie took part in a game of football, and Geri was pictured leaping up and down with joy, after which the two went to the most exclusive (and thus most talked-about) nightclub in the French resort.

And finally, Robbie broke his silence about the real nature of the relationship. Were they a couple? Of course not. 'We've been having such a laugh reading the stuff that has been written about us,' he said. 'We are not girlfriend and boyfriend and are not in love. We are just two people who have been through the same thing and each understands what the other has been thinking. She doesn't want to go out with me because I am too much of a slag.'

This, of course, did absolutely nothing to put a halt to the speculation: rather, it just started further rumours about whether they were actually playing a brilliant game of double bluff. If Robbie said they weren't in a relationship, the thinking went, then maybe we would believe him and leave them alone, which is want they want, because actually, they are in a relationship … Certainly, they showed no sign whatsoever of wanting to be left alone. If the two of them had issued daily press releases announcing exactly what they had in store for the day, they could not have attracted more attention than they did.

And it was a break Robbie needed. Quite apart from his feelings about Nicole – on one occasion, he announced, 'I wish her good luck – the bitch' – yet another long-running legal case had come to a head. Robbie finally settled a claim from Kevin Kinsella, his first manager after leaving Take That, a settlement that was estimated to have cost up to £500,000. 'At the time Robbie came to me for help he was in a bad way, and I told him I would sort his career out for him, which I did,' said an aggrieved Kinsella. 'But his mother changed her mind and decided that they didn't want to pay all the money for the work I'd done.'

Robbie continued to press the point that he and Geri were only friends. 'I like her an awful lot and don't want to ruin the friendship by it becoming more than that,' he said. 'I also want the press to be wrong. They think we're in love, blah, blah, blah. But she sleeps in that room and I'm over there. We haven't slept together or kissed. She's a really nice girl who I can't mess about. It's very difficult because she's beautiful, fantastic personality, sexy, but she's just my mate. I'm still sowing my seeds.'

It sounded as if Robbie was becoming slightly more mature. He admitted that he had been out with people and gone on to let them down. 'I've done that in the past and I want to grow up,' he said. 'If I had a daughter, I wouldn't allow her to go out with the person I am, but I'd allow her to go out with the person I'll become. My big thing is that I want to have kids and a family, even though I know it doesn't look that way. The future Mrs Williams is out there tonight, but it's like, "Stop looking". It's not going to happen because I couldn't handle commitment at the moment. I'd run a mile.'

It even seemed as if Robbie was beginning to come to terms with his status. 'This is the first proper holiday I've had in years – the others were booze trips where I went mental for a week and needed another holiday to recover,' he said. 'Now I sit back and go, "I'm a proper star", with a view of the south of France, a swimming pool, those trees, my driver Patrick and a chef. Is that not great?' And of the press attention, he conceded, 'I wouldn't be in this big villa if I hadn't done something. I'd be in bloody Scarborough getting pissed with my mates. So the sensible side of me says nothing is for free and you have to take the rough with the smooth. The other side wants to kick them in the nuts.'

But Robbie was a pro and knew that the publicity the trip had garnered was invaluable. He had a new album out that autumn, *Sing When You're Winning*, and its chances in the charts could not have been hurt by the fact that Robbie had spent most of the preceding summer on the front pages. In the event, it went to Number 1. Then there was another storm when his duet with Kylie was finally released because the song, 'Kids', ended with a rap containing the line, 'Press be asking do I care for sodomy? I don't know – yeah, probably.' (Kylie's record company cut the rap from the version of the song that appeared on her album.)

Robbie wasn't bothered – he was too busy posing naked, his back to the camera, with the supermodel Gisele, for the cover of the September issue of *Vogue*. He was only the third man in the past 30 years to appear on the cover of the magazine. *Top Of The Pops*, meanwhile, cut the offending line and the single ended up at Number 2.

But the split with Nicole continued to haunt Robbie, and he infuriated his ex when he publicly claimed never to have been in love with her. That was very much at odds with his past behaviour, but Nicole's relationship with Liam was becoming increasingly serious and Robbie no doubt felt the need to tell the world that he couldn't care less. Nicole lashed out, calling her ex a 'treacherous bastard'.

She also revealed that she had attended therapy sessions with him to try to wean him off drugs. 'I had to stand up and say, "Hi, I'm Nicole Appleton and my boyfriend has a problem,"' she said. 'It was really full on. I was shitting myself. It was scarring. It would never happen like that again. I'm not a sucker. I'm not going to pick up the pieces again. Go to fucking rehab clinics with them and fucking do all that … So. Cord is cut.' It certainly was. The two have scarcely had a good word to say about each other since – a sad ending for a couple who had once been so close.

But Robbie cheered himself up as he always had done – with adulation from his fans. He went on a 21-date tour in the autumn, one day appearing in a black jumpsuit and the next in jeans and a T-shirt, and always attracting massive acclaim. In November, he was nominated for five MTV Europe Awards, although he won only Best Song award for 'Rock DJ'. The win was overshadowed by the news that Nicole was pregnant with Liam's child.

Robbie started showing signs of stress again. He stormed out of the Q Awards in October close to tears, after Liam Gallagher called him 'queer'. One minute he would be dancing, quite literally, on the table; the next he was barely conscious. His behaviour at that year's MTV Europe Awards caused serious alarm. Although he wasn't feeling well, Robbie turned up and put in a rousing performance of 'Kids' with Kylie Minogue. He then went on to a party at the Grand Hotel, at one point dancing on the tables as he yelled, 'Party, party, I am the king. Now let's rock this place' – before he got into a set-to with record producer Nellee Hooper. He then collapsed shortly afterwards, foaming at the mouth, and had to be carried out. There were strenuous denials that he was drinking excessively again; rather he was said to be 'exhausted'. Reports circulated that he had gastro-enteritis, that he had flu, that he was being treated for sex addiction ...

Something had clearly gone very wrong. One fellow guest at the party, Andreas Lundberg, witnessed the whole incident. 'The party was well under way when Robbie jumped on the table with Wyclef Jean,' he said. 'He was wild eyed but seemed to be enjoying himself as they sang two songs together. He moved towards the crowds, who were all around him, cheering. One of them handed him a glass of beer. He took it and had a drink. Then he swayed a bit and all of a sudden Robbie fell down. No one had any idea what was happening. One minute he seemed lively and the next he collapsed. I caught a quick look at his face and he did not look very well. But no one could get near him. The bodyguards kept everyone away and rushed him out the back.'

Another person in the crowd was Jonathan Wilkes, who was earlier heard telling his friend, 'Come on, Rob, you've had enough, now.'

Although it was a frightening experience for everyone present, the party proved to be the wake-up call Robbie needed. Determined to sober himself up, he flew to Barbados, the scene of his 1996 holiday with Jacqui Hamilton-Smith, accompanied by Guy Chambers, and, after an initial temper tantrum at the hotel, he settled quietly down to recover. At the time of writing, he has not had a drink from that day onwards.

But the quiet did not last long. Back in Britain he gave an interview about his holiday with Geri saying that they didn't sleep together and 'I'm gay anyway', before outing himself for a second time during a concert in Paris. 'I have been in a steady sexual relationship for three years now,' he told astonished fans. 'So this is my coming-out party – I am now officially known as Roberta Williams.'

The record company, increasingly concerned by his behaviour, told Robbie to pipe down. Restarting the gay rumours of his own accord appeared to be commercial madness – after all, not everyone got the famed Williams sense of humour. Robbie did pipe down, albeit briefly – and 2001 was to prove his most successful year yet.

11
THE BANDWAGON
ROLLS ON

Whatever the truth about Robbie's condition at the end of 2000, he was clearly exhausted and needed some time to assess the future. In January 2001, he flew out to California to see what possibilities might be available to him. 'I need to get away and take a break from the music scene and London,' he said. 'I love it here and could happily live in Los Angeles. I haven't decided what I want to do but I think I want to give up the music. I want to become a movie star and LA is the place to do it.'

This was not music to the ears of Robbie's record company – and indeed, to date, Robbie is a singer, not an actor – but LA did offer him the opportunity to sort out his problems with more anonymity than he could ever find in London. Robbie decided to get his drinking under control (again) and signed up with the LA branch of Alcoholics Anonymous, which met at Crescent Heights Methodist Church in Hollywood. He also started looking into taking acting classes at the Lee Strasberg Theater Institute in New York.

It helped that he already had friends in the USA. Geri Halliwell was also spending time in LA, and so the two could meet up as regularly as they did in the UK. Robbie continued to scoff at talk of a romance, however. 'I couldn't give her what she deserves,' he said. 'We get together and talk about how bizarre our lives are. When we're with other people, Geri talks to everyone and that suits me because then I can just people watch. I'm socially inept, you see.'

That was a bit of an exaggeration, but Geri was helping Robbie with his recovery. She was helping him to avoid temptation and providing a shoulder to cry on when it all got too much. 'Robbie is always on his best behaviour when he's around Geri,' said a friend. 'He tones down his outrageous side. Geri's good for him because she doesn't drink or take drugs. Her only vice is smoking. Robbie also brings out Geri's mothering instincts. She cares for him a great deal and hates to see him unhappy or troubled. She's one of the few people who understands what he's going through – because she has experienced problems, too.'

Although he was to return to LA for a much longer stay, his commitments in Britain meant that Robbie had to return home in February. And all those signs that Robbie was coming to terms with himself were clearly red herrings. Robbie was, if anything, becoming even more depressed than he had been previously – and now it was the burden of fame that he found so hard to bear.

'It does my head in – everyone wants a piece of me,' he said. 'What would you say if I told you I sit inside crying behind the door because of my fame? Do you know, I'm the fourth most famous person in the country at the moment. That's not easy and it's caused me a lot of pain. I find it very hard to deal with. I can't walk down the street and I can't lead a normal life.' Poor Robbie. Couldn't live with fame; couldn't live without it – and to this day he has not found the ideal balance.

And, although a European tour was coming up, Robbie was serious about trying to break into acting. It was probably unwise to allow his name to become linked with the search for the next James Bond – the producers were hardly likely to choose someone with almost no acting experience, however much Robbie liked to see himself in the role, and indeed his agent, Sam Richards of Storm Artist Management, began playing it down. 'As far as James Bond is concerned, we haven't been offered it and Robbie considers Sean Connery to be the definitive Bond,' she said.

But other offers were coming in, too – and Robbie kept turning them down. He had already been offered roles in *Shaft*, starring Samuel L Jackson, *There's Only One Jimmy Grimble* with Robert Carlyle and *Tosspot* with Kathy Burke, but had said no to them all because of his singing commitments. In fact, the only role he had taken on, to date, was a one-off special of *The Fast Show*, to be screened on Red Nose Day in March. Doubts were beginning to surface as to whether Robbie really was serious about a change in career, not least because it would mean starting at the bottom again. 'When we find something that really excites him, we'll go for it,' said Sam. 'A lot of the roles that come his way are the cheeky chappie-type character. But Robbie's keen to do something quite dark and serious, which is why *Shaft* so appealed to him.'

Nor did he seem to be on the verge of leaving London. Robbie was spending £2 million on renovating his new house: putting a recording studio in the basement, a huge sitting room on the ground floor and a vast bedroom suite for himself, including a dressing room and bathroom. 'He loves popping in to see how things are getting on and he's itching to move in,' said a friend. 'He spends his time running around like a child, imagining what everything will look like.' Nor was that his only tie to London: Robbie had also invested a tidy sum in a new club called Century in central London, with the restaurateur Pierre Condou.

Jonathan Wilkes continued to play a very important role in Robbie's life, and Robbie explained why. 'I have to go to places that are exclusive and expensive to protect myself,' he said. 'I can't go to the pub. Well, I can, but I'll get hassled all night and ruin everyone's evening. Not many 26-year-olds go to the places I go, so I don't get the chance to make friends.' Nor was it a coincidence that Jonathan's mother was a great friend of Jan's. Jonathan came from where Robbie came from – and was very unlikely ever to spill the beans on his friend's hedonistic lifestyle.

Not that Robbie wished to continue with his hedonism. As he made plans to embark on his European tour, he climbed on the wagon yet again – but this time he was determined to stay there. Calling a meeting with everyone who would be going on the tour with him, he asked that there would be no drinking and drug taking when he was around, as he found it too hard to cope. This scene and a great deal more of the tour is captured on the documentary *Nobody Someday*, which in turn presents a picture of a young man in turmoil. Still only 27, Robbie had been famous for over a decade and it showed. In the documentary he complains constantly about his fame, claiming that he didn't enjoy any of it any more, that he hated going out on stage and that his life was miserable.

It must be said that, since then, Robbie himself has expressed surprise about how gloomy he seemed, and these claims are set against footage of him in concert, where he makes a very good stab at appearing to enjoy himself, if he was really as downbeat as he seemed. He also has the good grace to admit that having a lot of money was not without its benefits. Nevertheless, he was clearly feeling unhappy.

It was also a picture of quite how far Robbie's life had come to differ from that of his fans. As lackeys swarmed around him, cutting his hair and polishing up his appearance, his personal assistant explained that everything had to be done to keep the great man happy, and that Robbie's entourage had to do everything, right down to ensuring there was food in his fridge. Robbie might have become too arrogant of late but there are very few young men who would be able to stay normal when they are on the receiving end of that kind of attention. If Robbie thinks too much of himself, then he is, by a long shot, not the only one responsible.

And his fame was putting Robbie in some increasingly unpleasant situations. He was becoming more and more paranoid about security – and not without reason. Early on in the tour as Robbie was playing a concert in Stuttgart, he was attacked by a mentally ill member of the audience. As he launched into the encore at the Schleyer Hall, the 20-year-old 'psychologically disturbed' fan jumped on to the stage, punched Robbie, and hurled him five feet into a pit in front of the audience, before being restrained by security staff.

'He told us that the Robbie Williams on stage was not the real one but a doppelganger,' said Dieter Topel of the Stuttgart police. 'A member of the band, the guitarist, tried to seize the attacker, and in the struggle the attacker also fell into the security area, where he was held by security staff. He was arrested and taken to see a doctor. He is severely disturbed and has a history of mental illness.'

At first, the audience couldn't work out what was happening. 'This guy rushed on to the stage and grabbed Robbie,' said fan Ulrika Sanger, who was there on the night. 'I thought it was part of the act, but then I saw them struggling and the music stopped.'

Robbie was extremely shocked and in pain, but clambered back on to the stage and announced: 'We can't let an idiot like that spoil our joy tonight. I'm carrying on for you.' He was greeted with a massive round of applause and cheers at his bravery – and it really was bravery, as he was more shocked than he let on. 'He was very depressed back at his hotel and wasn't seeing anybody,' said Ulrich Bauer, a reporter from the *Stuttgart Nachrichten*. 'He is just so puzzled as to why someone he doesn't know would want to hurt him like this.

'I was there and it was shocking. The man just seemed to push Robbie into space. There was no provocation. He seemed to come from nowhere. Robbie was rubbing his arm when he reappeared. It was clear he was very shocked but he is a great performer. When the crowd went wild as he got back on stage, he performed with even more emotion than he had done before.'

Unsurprisingly, Robbie stepped up security after that. He returned to Britain for the Brit Awards, requesting that his table be kept alcohol free, and performed a rousing rendition of 'Rock DJ' flanked by giant-sized Brit Awards and semi-naked dancers. He also scooped another three himself, bringing his total tally to 12. One of these, 'Best British Male Solo Artist', was presented by Geri Halliwell, who had shrunk even further and was putting a good deal of what remained of her on show in a mini skirt and micro top. 'He is very male, he is very healthy and, according to the press, he has been giving me one, so now I'm going to give him one: my very dear friend, Robbie Williams,' she chirped, handing over the award.

Robbie accepted the award gracefully and mentioned the previous year, when he'd had a go at Liam Gallagher. 'I normally stand up here saying something stupid like challenging someone to a fight,' he said. 'But not this year. I am going to say nothing but thank you all.'

Next up was the Best British Video for 'Rock DJ'. 'You will have to excuse the big security presence with me,' said Robbie on accepting the award. 'It's not that I am getting all big time. It's just that someone might try and throw me off the stage.'

And finally, there was the Best Single for 'Rock DJ'. 'I feel like the most loved person in the world,' said a clearly moved Robbie. 'People have nothing but smiles and handshakes and "Nice one, Robbie" comments for me. There seems to be nothing but love and it's cool. It's really cool.' But recent strains had taken their toll. 'I'm not putting an album out next year,' Robbie went on. 'I'm taking some time out to find myself. I've been spending a lot of time at home, playing cards, eating chocolate and chilling with a few friends. It's good for my head.'

The newly sober and mature Robbie skipped the parties that night – and then turned up on Capital Radio the next day to complain about how boring awards ceremonies are. 'They're pants. They're real, real pants,' he said rather ungraciously, before going on to moan about how far his table was from the stage. But again, Robbie was reassessing his priorities. The night before he had dedicated the Best British Video Award to his four-and-a-half-month-old nephew, Freddie. Family was clearly on his mind as his sister Sally revealed.

'I had no idea he would dedicate an award to Freddie, it is a wonderful thing to do,' she said. 'We were talking on the telephone shortly before the ceremony and discussing what we thought was truly important in life. Robbie and I agreed that the most important thing is your family and friends. It is especially important for someone in the music business like Robbie. It doesn't matter how successful you are or how famous, what really counts is your relationships with those that are closest to you. Robbie is so proud at becoming an uncle for the first time. He absolutely adores Freddie.'

One of Robbie's companions that night at the Brits was Jonathan Wilkes, who was continuing to try to break into the business himself. But still speculation surrounded the real nature of the relationship. Despite the continuing presence of Geri in his life, Robbie did not have a steady girlfriend and rumour persisted that he and Jonathan were more than just friends. Jonathan laughed it off.

'It's just one of those things where I am very fortunate, in a way, that my best friend is top of the tree in his industry and it's the one I want to go into,' he said. 'He's just like my best mate. We are like brothers. I love living there. We come home and go, "Hi pop star!" "Hi pop star!" It's Pop Star Towers. We just have a laugh, do what any 22-year-old and 27-year-old would do. We drink tea, play computers, watch telly, play pool and play football. There aren't any house rules and there's usually music playing all the time. There tend to be trainers and clothes left around all the time – it's a busy place with lots of people coming and going. A restaurant is our canteen.'

This did little to dispel suspicions. Robbie was a multi-millionaire by now, observers noted, and how many multi-millionaires have flatmates? But that was to miss several points. For a start, despite all his success, Robbie was still relatively immature and liked indulging in the laddish behaviour that he'd all but had to give up in his late teens. And secondly, Jonathon is one of only three people – the others are Jan and Sally – who provide a link between the world of his childhood and the world he lives in today. Robbie had found it impossible to stay in touch with his old friends from Stoke, simply because they were in awe of who he had become, while at the same time his new showbiz friends led him into a world of temptations that he found it very hard to resist. He was also beginning to develop the caution towards newcomers that many very famous people have, simply because he doubted their motives. With Jonathon, there was never anything to doubt. He knew Robbie as a child, he knows Robbie now and the two are friends. That was all there was to it.

Ironically, for someone who complained so much about losing his privacy, Robbie signed an £800,000 book deal to collaborate with the writer Mark McCrum on a book entitled *Somebody, Someday* to tell the story behind the 2001 tour. He was nearly poached from EMI by BMG in a seven-figure deal, before EMI grabbed him back again. And he was heading back on stage to continue the European leg of the tour. But his fears about his own security were heightened when Geri's flat was broken into. It was near his own house in Notting Hill and, although he was already having extensive security devices installed, it made him upgrade once again.

'Geri phoned Robbie after her break-in,' said one of Robbie's entourage. 'She was in a terrible way. It made Robbie realise how vulnerable he was to an attack from any deranged nut on the street. The break-in has rammed home to Robbie he can't spend too much money on home security. He already planned on having CCTV and alarms. Now the security is going to be much tighter – especially around the walls of the garden, which will be alive with trip switches and infra-red beams.'

The break-in happened when Robbie was on holiday in Tenerife, but he gallantly flew home to cheer up Geri. This, of course, fuelled more rumours about him and Geri. Robbie seemed determined to spread disinformation: twice he said that he and Geri are friends who sleep together and twice he then said he hadn't really meant it. Then he announced he was gay. Then he said that he wore his tiger underpants when the two of them were in bed together.

No one knew exactly what the truth was, but this marked the beginning of the end for the friendship. Geri was enjoying renewed career success herself with her cover of 'It's Raining Men', which featured in the film *Bridget Jones's Diary*, and she was not pleased to hear Robbie talking so openly about their relationship. 'Robert visits here,' she said, pointing at her head on the *Graham Norton* show, 'and here,' her heart, 'but not there.' She pointed downwards.

'You're not having sex then?' asked a disappointed Graham. 'No,' said Geri.

For all his contradictions, Robbie was genuinely trying to give something back to the society that had made him so famous. After meeting leukaemia patient Johanna MacVicar in Glasgow, Robbie appealed for bone marrow donors to come forward, prompting a response from nearly 1,000 men. It was also at this time that Robbie donated the £165,000 raised from an auction of his belongings to help Stoke-on-Trent. It broke his heart to see what was happening to his old city, said Robbie, adding, 'A factory seems to be closed or knocked down every day – these are buildings I saw as a child.' He also donated money to his old school, St Margaret Ward RC High.

The people of Stoke certainly appreciated it. Louise Tierney, a former head girl of St Margaret, who went on to work with children, said, 'It's brilliant – he's a role model for so many kids round here. He might encourage others to take pride in the area because he does. I'm not surprised he's done this. I know he's kept in touch with the school. He had a bit of a run-in with a careers teacher who said he wouldn't get anywhere, but he hasn't held that against them.'

And the struggle for sobriety went on. Like so many people who give up alcohol, Robbie was suffering from insomnia. 'I can't get to sleep nowadays until 5 o'clock in the morning,' he complained. 'I used to be able to sleep really easily with the aid of alcohol. Now I'm off it, I'm trying to get lots of fresh air and knacker myself out playing football.'

By this time, the rift with Geri was becoming public. Robbie had claimed again that he wore his tiger-decorated Y-fronts in bed with her, prompting her to assert, 'I am out with Robbie Williams a lot, but he is NOT my boyfriend and we are NOT a couple.' The two then totally ignored one another at the Capital FM awards – and that despite sitting at the same table.

There were rumours that Geri was jealous of a fling Robbie had with Rod Stewart's daughter Kimberly.

Robbie tried to placate her. In an appearance on the *Parkinson* show he told the audience he loved Geri. He sent her presents of clothing and jewellery to try to make up. But he had gone too far. Geri was particularly angry about a remark he'd made on Radio 1 – 'Geri and I are just good friends who have the occasional shag' – and was not backing down. The friendship was over. 'I can't stand men in tight, tiny underpants with animal designs on them,' she said coolly. 'I prefer blokes in a cute pair of boxer shorts. I find that much more attractive. Robbie is a real turn off in those things, but he would try anything for a laugh.'

It was a shame. Geri had brought some stability to Robbie's life and had encouraged him to stay healthy. Now, bereft of her influence, all the old insecurities returned. Confessing to being haunted by 'internal demons', he continued, 'If your time is up, your time is up. If they want to come and get you, they will come and get you. I don't know who "they" are.'

But Robbie's paranoia was hardly surprising. After the incident in Germany, he was badly shaken again during a visit to LA – which was increasingly becoming his home from home – when a stranger left a voicemail on his hotel phone saying, 'We were meant to be together for eternity. I'll be paying you a visit soon.' For someone who was already nervous about his personal safety, it was almost the last straw. Robbie swapped his open-topped car for a Range Rover, and beefed up his security presence. 'This is getting a tad ridiculous,' he said wearily. 'The reason that I love coming to LA is that I can go around without causing a scene. But anyone who's surrounded by a team of bodyguards is going to attract attention – and that's exactly what I'm doing. Even people who don't recognise me are staring at me. It's making me a nervous wreck.'

But he had to get on with the business of being a pop star. Robbie's next single was due out: a cover version of Queen's 'We Are The Champions'. There was even talk of Robbie teaming up with Queen and stepping into the shoes of Freddie Mercury, the Queen vocalist who died in 1991, before everyone involved came to their senses. Then came the single 'Eternity', which referred to a summer spent holidaying with a beautiful woman … Robbie eventually revealed who the song was about. 'A lot of people think this song is for Gary Barlow – but it's not. It's for the little yoga girl.'

But there really was no going back with Geri. She had given several more interviews, point-blank denying that there was anything between her and Robbie. It was clear that the friendship was over. Geri's ex-colleague in the Spice Girls Mel B added her bit when asked if all five of them had dated Robbie:

'Oh God, no,' she yelled. 'Neither Emma, Victoria nor I have gone out with him. Anyway, he prefers men.' One of Robbie's spokesmen promptly issued a denial.

But the speculation continued, to the extent that

Jonathan Wilkes responded to Mel in public. 'I think it was well out of order,' he said. 'It was kids' TV and, as a mum, she should know better when and where to shoot her mouth off. Everyone has been saying since year dot that there is something going on between Rob and me. We ignore it. Rob doesn't want to get in a slanging match – he's never said anything bad about her, so she should keep her mouth tightly buttoned. He's always said record sales speak for themselves. Maybe she should look after her business and leave Rob to look after his. She's just sad.'

There was consolation to be found elsewhere. For the third year in a row, *Company* readers voted Robbie the world's sexiest man, one ahead of Brad Pitt. And as summer approached, he headed back to the south of France, except this time with a group of male friends, including Jonathan, rather than Geri. They were clearly there to party. 'They've been having a real bachelor boys vacation, playing games on the beach and racing mopeds,' said one onlooker. 'Robbie's pretty famous in France and he and his pals had fun in attracting a lot of attention – especially from the girls.'

Robbie himself was only too happy to talk about girls. In a promo video for 'Eternity', which was a double A-side with 'Road to Mandalay', he boasts about his penchant for group sex. 'The only thing I love more than shagging two birds at one time is life itself,' he announces. The message was clear. Robbie likes sleeping with women – not men.

But he didn't like Geri any more. From the tone of the interviews she'd been giving, it was quite clear that the friendship was over. Now Robbie decided it was time to retaliate and, just as he had with Nicole Appleton, he decided after the event that it was he who had tired of Geri rather than vice versa. 'She turned into a demonic little girl playing with dolls and a tea set,' he said in an interview with the *Sunday Times*. 'She started speaking like a psychotic child and she developed this possessed look in her eye. It was genuinely scaring me.

'She was OK – mad but good mad – before she was working, but when her career began happening again she became a different person. Making these manic, impulsive decisions. It was around that time I realised that our friendship wasn't what I thought it was.' Did he miss her? 'No, I don't,' said Robbie harshly. 'I'd be lying if I said I did.' Did they have sex? 'We slept together. I don't think we found each other physically attractive. It wasn't really a sex thing.'

He might not have had Geri, but Robbie did have the perfect rock star pad. Renovations had been completed and the house decorated in some style: the sunken front room, known as the 'conversation pit' houses an enormous 16-seater sofa and sound system, including a television the size of a cinema screen. An aquarium runs along one wall, behind which is a black and silver pool table. 'It's made out of platinum,' said Jonathan Wilkes to the *Sunday Times*. 'Rob went into the shop in

New York and asked the bloke how much it was. And, because Rob's just in jeans, the bloke looked at him and said, "It's out of your price bracket, buddy." Rob's like, "I was just wondering how much a pool table like that cost." All casual. So the bloke, who is now getting a bit annoyed, says, "It's a quarter of a million dollars, OK?" Rob goes, "I'll take it. Have it shipped over." Slaps down the credit card and walks outside to have a fag while they sort out the paperwork. How cool was that? I'll tell you, the bloke's expression was priceless. It was worth spending all that on a pool table just to see his face.'

The rest of the house is similarly elegant. A blue glass staircase runs through the house, going from Robbie's office, where his awards are neatly lined up, up to the bedroom suite with its huge bathroom, also equipped with a television screen, and leather-covered walk-in wardrobe. Original artwork covers the walls. In an interview, Robbie once admitted, 'If I fall asleep here in the afternoon, I wake up and the first thing that enters my head is, "I don't deserve this." But when I think about it, I've worked so bloody hard that I must deserve some of it.'

By July, Robbie was on the Irish and European leg of his tour. 'Eternity' was at Number 1 and, such was the gold of his touch, tone of the most bizarre requests yet came through: the Scottish Tourist Board wanted to film (English) Robbie in a kilt in order to boost the Scottish tourism industry. 'We would point out that his tour schedule is hectic,' said a spokesperson for Robbie as she politely turned down the request.

And Robbie had something much more ambitious in mind. He had grown up listening to the classics and had always loved the music of the 1940s and 1950s: now he was thinking about doing something with those songs. The first hint of what was to come came from Guy Chambers. 'Have you heard what Rob wants to do?' he was overheard saying at a party. 'He wants to record an album of Sinatra songs. He's serious about it. Selected the songs himself, knows them inside out and he really can sing that stuff. It was like he was born to it.'

In many ways he was. Robbie had never entirely resolved his complicated relationship with his father, but one of the ways the two had always communicated was through music. Robbie had proved himself as a pop star and a rock star many times over, but now he wanted to step up a league. He wanted to take on the greats, sing the greats and put himself up there with the greats. And if, in so doing, he wanted to prove himself to his father, he was about to do so. And then some.

12
ROBBIE SINGS SINATRA

When it came to singing Sinatra, Robbie had form. Not only had he grown up singing the classics, he had also recorded the number 'Have You Met Miss Jones' for the smash hit film *Bridget Jones's Diary*. Now, he was determined that his new venture would be a success: as well as recording a new album, *Swing When You're Winning*, he would also play London's Royal Albert Hall for a one-off concert. And he would record a duet. With Nicole Kidman.

Like Robbie, Nicole regularly topped polls citing her as one of the most beautiful people in the world. And, like Robbie, she was single. The former Mrs Tom Cruise had learned that her marriage was over earlier in the year, and what better consort for one of the world's most famous pop stars than one of the world's most famous actresses? On top of that, she could even sing, as witnessed by her appearance in the film *Moulin Rouge*.

The prospect excited everyone and took Robbie's mind off other matters, not least the fact that the United States had yet to succumb to his charms. For all his regular trips to the States, for all his concerts and television appearances, he was still getting nowhere. In fact, Robbie was becoming so fed up with his failure to impact on the American consciousness that he was beginning to say he would not be releasing any more records in the States. Some people blamed his arrogance for his failure to crack the Stars and Stripes nut; others said he simply had to work harder. 'Robbie tours a lot elsewhere, but not in America,' said the singer Usher. 'US fans like to get up close and personal. They want to feel loved by their idols. That takes time, so you have to work at it.'

Others thought that Robbie came across as too English, amongst them the 18-year-old Irish singer Samantha Mumba, who had already made it in America. 'People say how can someone like Robbie Williams not make it in America and you can?' she said. 'But Robbie is very English – and so is his humour. I think a lot of American audiences don't get that tongue-in-cheek humour thing that he does. I'm a very different act from Robbie. It's a combination of my background and what I'm about and somehow people seem to love it in America.'

His romantic life wasn't going that smoothly either.

Robbie was making his usual headway through models, air stewardesses, groupies and actresses, but there was no one serious. He was briefly linked to the model Lisa Marie, before heading off in pursuit of another, Lisa Seiffert, who appeared with him on the video for 'Eternity'. But she wasn't interested in him. 'I think Robbie's great but I haven't got time for a boyfriend at the moment,' she said. He was then linked with Rita Simmons of Girls@Play but that also came to nothing.

And, as ever when Robbie was under stress, there was the inevitable strip. After a concert in Germany, he went to the Rheinterrassen restaurant in Cologne and gave fellow guests something to feast their eyes on, as well. 'The party was really boring at first,' said fellow partygoer Tine Steinacker. 'There were a couple of minor German celebrities lounging around at the bar and it seemed as if Robbie wasn't going to show.' He did and started singing 'Rock DJ'. 'Robbie slowly circled his hips around, then pulled his T-shirt off,' Tina continued. 'Then he took his jeans down and stood there just in his pants, just like in the video. And he didn't stop there. He pulled his pants down and stood there naked. Holding his hands in front of his jewels, he hopped across the dance floor. What a superstar!'

He certainly had a packed schedule. Immediately after finishing his European tour, Robbie was due in LA, where he was going to record the new album. Then it was back to Blighty for a concert, along with a tour of Australia, New Zealand and South-East Asia. At the same time the documentary team that had been following him for the past five months were putting the finishing touches to the film – some critics who hadn't been keeping abreast of the turn of events were surprised that Geri made no appearance in the film – after which Robbie was planning a long rest. 'Robbie's moving to LA within months,' said a friend. 'He's determined to make it as a TV star.'

And so Robbie flew to LA for the first visit, to record the album. He was working at the legendary Capitol Studios, no less, the very same studios Frank Sinatra used. 'I've loved this music since I was a kid,' Robbie said, as he prepared to start recording. 'This is me doffing my cap to the Rat Pack. For me to sing in front of the band that backed Sinatra in the same studio that he used is an honour. Prepare to be astonished.'

And, of course, there was the duet with Nicole Kidman. The two were to sing 'Somethin' Stupid', the song originally made famous when Frank duetted with his daughter Nancy. 'Nicole has a beautiful voice,' said an awestruck Robbie. 'I heard her sing in *Moulin Rouge* and I asked if she would be interested, fully expecting to be knocked back – she's a proper Hollywood star. But she said yes. I was amazed and thrilled.'

For her part, Nicole was serene. 'He is a total pleasure to work with,' she said. 'He put me at my ease and made me laugh. Now I'm seriously thinking of getting a tattoo like his. Robbie is a sweet soul and a great singer. His version of "Mr Bojangles" made me cry.'

But Robbie just couldn't stop being Robbie. Just as eager tongues were linking him to one of the most desirable women in the world – Nicole – yet again he started the gay rumours. On *Top Of The Pops* in April, he told the audience, 'Tomorrow I will be coming out as a homosexual – so get in there while you can, girls.' This time round he managed to attend an AA meeting for gay men. 'It was awkward at first but once I relaxed it was actually very helpful,' said Robbie. 'In fact, I had such a good time I'll probably attend another of their meetings.'

Nothing could detract from his enjoyment of what he was doing, though. Robbie even managed to get a complaint called 'Swing Finger', brought on by snapping his fingers as he sang. 'This is the most fun I have ever had from recording,' he chortled. 'My only complaint is that my fingers are sore from clicking them – I'm suffering from swing finger.'

And the friendship with Nicole continued. Both were giving interviews about the duet in which both cooed with praise for the other. Asked about the recording, Nicole said, 'We did it very quickly one afternoon. But I have no desire to be a singer. I just did it for fun. I think he's very talented and I had a giggle. We're both extremely busy but we're making time to get to know each other better, and I'm very happy about that.' Friends of Nicole spoke of Robbie as a 'shoulder to cry on' after her split from Tom Cruise, adding he was 'just what the doctor ordered'.

Back in London, Robbie was indulging in more eccentric behaviour. Earlier in the year, he had held a party when he moved into his new home and several of the female guests had turned up wearing Robbie Williams masks. Robbie, bizarrely, began to do the same thing, wandering around London disguised as himself. If it was a ploy to attract attention, it worked. The book *Somebody, Someday* was also due out, while, with perfect timing, Robbie won the GQ Award for Solo Artist of the Year.

With hindsight, it is clear that Robbie was becoming increasingly exhausted. Apart from the odd holiday, he had been working flat out for four years now and badly needed a rest. On top of that, Robbie himself was well aware he had a vulnerable streak and could start behaving oddly with very little provocation – hence the frequent striptease. 'I always fancied being a bit mad – I like to think of myself as an eccentric,' he confessed. 'Weird people are interesting. So I prayed for that and got it. Now I don't have full control over what I do, and it's scary. I've got a terrifying, warped perception of the world. I haven't had reality for 10 years. Now I can't find my own reality that I'm happy in, or one that isn't full of shame and regrets. Everyone has their demons. I'm a split personality, a psychologist's dream – part of my character is very self-destructive.'

But Robbie soon found diversions to lift him out of himself again, not least Nicole Kidman. The actress was in London on a visit and the two lost no time in renewing their acquaintance, with Nicole going round to Robbie's house for dinner. 'It's clear that Nicole has got the hots for Robbie, and she just wanted to be with him, with no one else around,' said a friend. 'They had an early evening meal together at his place but I don't believe she stayed the night.'

Actually, very little was clear about what was really going on. Robbie and Nicole both had reasons for making it appear that they were interested in one another: it publicised their new single and presumably irritated Tom Cruise. Robbie had seen the blanket press coverage he got when duetting with Kylie Minogue and then talking about how attracted he was to her – now he and Nicole were doing much the same thing.

In some ways, sex seemed to have replaced drink and drugs in Robbie's mind. He was as active as ever, even if the future Mrs Williams was nowhere in sight, telling Radio 1, 'My sexual appetite is no more or no less than any other 27-year-old, but I have someone to go down and pick girls for me. We're going to get a webcam so I can stay and watch from my hotel room while someone goes and finds the girls. I can direct them, "Go down to the feet."'

It seems unlikely that Nicole ever became one of those girls, but both were wise enough to keep people guessing, especially when the record company chose the duet as a single which, in due course, went to Number 1. 'It's a great song and we reckon it's a smash,' said a spokesman. 'They sound great together – it sends shivers down the spine.'

Robbie was almost bashful about it. 'She was really shy,' he confided as he recalled the recording session. 'And I was dead shy anyway, because she was coming into the studio. I was really shy and nervous. Then she arrived and she was shy and nervous, and I just took all her shyness and all her nerves as well and it was like a double whammy. I was falling asleep I was that nervous. But she was wonderful.'

But Nicole was not the only person Robbie duetted with on the album. He also recorded a song with Rupert Everett, one of the few actors in Hollywood who is openly gay. Robbie acknowledged this. 'We've recorded "Can't Take That Away From Me", a big gay ballad,' he said brightly. Speculation intensified, yet again, as to the true nature of Robbie's sexuality.

One person who kept a concerned eye on him from afar was another gay star, Sir Elton John. 'Robbie I keep my eye on from a distance,' he said in an interview at the time. 'I worry about him but he seems to be doing all right. I always feel he's a bit of a loose cannon. He has that look in his eye. Robbie's still very, very young – he's only 27, and can't have a drink, and that scares him, you can see. He has that self-destruct button which we all have but he wears it on his sleeve.

'He has self-esteem problems and he seems to hate himself. He has cemented himself as the number one male artist in Britain. But he's like a little deer caught in the headlights. I love him. Underneath that frightened exterior is a sweetheart. In some ways he reminds me of myself when I was younger, though I had much more confidence than him. I mean, he's confident on stage but I wasn't a jittery wreck off it.'

Despite all the turmoil, though, the numerous teases about his sexuality, his choice of girlfriends and his mental health, Robbie was beginning to show some signs of coming to terms with his past. He was even beginning to regret the numerous jibes aimed at his old colleagues in Take That – and that, for Robbie, was a massive step forward.

'I saw one of those programmes the other night – *I Love 1993* – and there was a big piece on it about Take That,' he said. 'It really upset me: really, really upset me. Howard and Mark were speaking and they just looked really sad about the whole thing. You could see it in their eyes. I just went in my back garden and had a cry. We were all really young when we were subjected to this mad world, this phenomenon. It was very instant and very big. And that, sort of, messes with people's heads. It has with mine and I know it has with theirs. I have been very bitter about stuff. I'm sorry about what I've said about any of the parties concerned. It is a public apology, I suppose.' It is said that only by forgiving past slights can you move forward. By making that apology, Robbie was also showing that he had forgiven his old bandmates for what he saw as their hurtful treatment of him. He was at long last ready to move forward.

He was also ready to perform his new style, the big band style, live – and in October, he did just that. He had taken over the Royal Albert Hall for the occasion, with Rupert Everett on hand as a compere and Jane Horrocks accompanying him in one duet, but there was no question that it was Robbie's night. Dressed in suit and tie, à la Rat Pack, Robbie sang in front of a big band, a group of backing singers and a giant RW made out of light bulbs. According to the BBC, however, while Sinatra might have been The Voice, Robbie was still merely The Tonsils from Tunstall – albeit ones which laid on a good show. He hadn't lost his sense of humour, either, referring to himself as Ol' Big Head.

In many ways, the concert was really Robbie pretending to be one of the original Rat Pack – its other members included Dean Martin, Sammy Davis Jnr and Peter Lawford – just as he had pretended to be James Bond in the 'Millennium' video. The sense that he was acting out some personal fantasy intensified with his finale which was, natch, 'My Way', before Robbie turned to a figure in the stalls. 'Mum,' said Robbie, 'this is your son singing.' It was handkerchiefs all round.

Except that it wasn't. Robbie might have been pretending to be Frank Sinatra for the night, but underneath he was still Robbie Williams and he just could not let the evening pass without creating some sort of controversy. And so it was the he did another duet – with none other than Jonathan Wilkes. The two sang 'Me and My Shadow', after which Wilkes begged

Robbie to allow him to stay on stage. 'If you let us sing again, I'll give you some money,' he said. 'I'll make you a cup of tea … I won't tell anyone you're gay!' In case anyone missed the point, there was also a huge sign above the duo's heads reading 'Rob and Jonny: They're Just Good Friends (Honest)'.

It had the desired effect: it created uproar. 'It's the biggest question in showbiz,' gossiped one industry insider, clearly thrilled that the subject had come up yet again. 'Everyone is always spreading rumours, asking questions. As for Robbie, one minute he's announcing on stage he's gay, the next he's telling the world about the women he's slept with.'

A weary spokeswoman for Robbie chipped in. 'He's not gay,' she said. 'He is straight. He just likes winding people up.'

He was not entirely adverse to the publicity it created, either. 'I don't give a toss if people think I'm gay,' he said once. 'I wouldn't say I've not thought about it, because you do. People do when they're growing up. I snogged a bloke once, but it wasn't a proper gay thing. I kissed him but it didn't float my boat.'

For the record, Jonathan Wilkes has a girlfriend.

Nor had Robbie forgotten about Nicole Kidman. Their single was due to be released that Christmas and so the two were reunited to make a video. There was a great deal of speculation as to what this video would entail, given that it was to be shot on a closed set – 'It's going to be hugely romantic!' said a source. What everyone really wanted to know, of course, was whether Nicole Kidman would take her clothes off. (In the event, the video was quite tastefully done.) On top of that, Robbie was spotted leaving her hotel in the early hours of the morning, prompting even more gossip.

'All his friends reckon something is going on, although Rob is keeping very quiet about the situation,' said a friend of the singer. 'He's certainly seemed happier over the last few weeks and we reckon Nicole has something to do with it. They have met several times since she has been in London and they get on fantastically. Both of them are massive flirts, they are both gorgeous and they are also both single. After all, Robbie's Britain's most eligible bachelor and she is one of the most beautiful women in the world.'

If the two were out to provoke the gossip, they couldn't have done better, with their behaviour during the making of the video giving rise to even more talk. 'Robbie and Nicole were fooling around like a couple of love-struck school kids – throwing fake snowballs and playing with St Bernard dogs,' said a source. 'We had to do a fair few retakes. Robbie won't confirm if anything's going on, but everyone could see the chemistry. They were laughing and giggling. They seemed inseparable.' The air of innocent romance was only slightly marred when two lap dancers confessed to enjoying a threesome with Robbie. After all, a guy's gotta do …

Of course, there were hints all along that both were

playing it up for all it was worth, while actually remaining nothing but friends. 'It's not what people might think,' Nicole admitted, 'but Robbie is irresistible because he is so much fun to be around. He's a very funny man. He also gives me amazing confidence ... Robbie and I have become good friends – and that's all.'

As autumn drew in, Robbie was up to his old antics. As usual, he dropped his trousers at a concert in Singapore, before asking the country's police force not to arrest him. He also upset some fans. 'I saw him when he came with his entourage for his soundcheck at the Singapore Indoor Stadium,' said one. 'He is the most snobbish, arrogant person I've ever seen. Maybe he wasn't in a good mood. Anyways, he expects people to treat him like a king. While he was playing with his soccer ball, everyone had to pick up the stray ball for him. Robster, I like your songs, but not you, man.'

Robbie flew on to Bangkok where – again in concert – he simulated sex with a life-size cut out of Kylie Minogue, after telling everyone how boring Singapore was. By November he was in Australia, and it was here that he really began to talk about plans for the New Year. Big changes were on the cards. Robbie had been thinking about taking time out for some time and now he was finally going to do it.

'I just find the whole thing, the whole "Robbie Williams" thing very boring,' he said. 'If I don't get a challenge then I get bored, and subsequently the shows suffer. I think that, after Australia, you'll see the last of Robbie Williams. I'm going to have some time off after that, and I might think differently. But I think I will probably kill him off.'

Always one to create a problem for himself if none was already on offer, Robbie was now complaining that, since he had proved himself as a solo artist, he needed something new. 'I think the struggle is a lot more fascinating, wanting to prove yourself is a lot more fascinating and rewarding than actually making it,' he said. 'I'm just about to go on stage at a stadium where 60,000 people have bought a ticket to see me. And that's what I wanted, but I've done it now.'

Robbie went on to say that he needed time off to see how he reacted and whether or not he would want to go back on stage. 'It'd be great to think that my ego doesn't need this much pampering,' he said in a rather revealing remark, 'and I could just slink off into the background and write shows or write stuff for other people or put other bands together. It would be nice to think I didn't need this. When I see U2 in concert, they're amazing. It baffles me how people keep this up for any length of time and why. Why? What's the point after a while?'

Robbie was also scared – scared of the performing and scared of what would happen if he walked away. 'I'm not here to be entertained tonight – they are,' he said of the audience at his shows. 'The most important thing to me is that they're going to go home really happy and inspired. That's what my job is. I pretty much bet they will all go home happy. As far as I'm concerned, it's too big. Playing stadiums is a bit scary. It really is. I'm scared. I was last week; I am now. But in this business, it's supply and demand. This many people want to see you play. Well, I've always been so insecure that everyone's going to leave that I've put out three albums in three and a half years. George Michael put out three in 10 years. But me, I haven't stopped working in 11 years. I need a break.'

He certainly did. That arrogant streak was coming increasingly to the fore, his mooning was becoming tiresome, and even Robbie was beginning to regret making quite such an issue about his sexuality. Asked why he kept outing himself on stage, he replied, 'Because I don't know how many times I've actually said what my sexuality is, and exactly how it doesn't really matter. Somebody asked me, "Why do you keep playing around with your sexuality and why don't you just come out with what you are?" I said I'll come out when I'm good and ready. I find the whole thing boring. That's why I make a joke of it. Why not? What's more interesting, me going "I'm straight" or me going "I might be gay"?' And the truth is? 'Look, I'm straight, all right? Fucking hell! Tell the world. What's wrong with it? Sorry, everyone. I tried being gay but it just wasn't for me! If I could take a gay pill now, I would. But I'm just not.'

Having cleared that up, Robbie revealed quite how

tedious he was beginning to find the whole business of concerts. Asked if he liked touring America and Australia, where he was not so well known, he replied, 'It's great. The expectancy level is not that high. The people in England know what to expect. In Australia or America they don't. I love the look on their faces when people aren't sure what's happening. Halfway through they like it, by the end they're going, "This is fucking ace." To me the most rewarding gigs I've done have been in front of 400 people who haven't got a fucking clue what's going to happen. In England, people know. They know they'll bounce about in "Let Me Entertain You", they'll sing back to me. I'll do this; they'll do that. I much prefer winning people over than actually winning.'

There was an added bonus to touring Australia that autumn: Nicole Kidman, who was in the country promoting her film *The Others*. There were signs, however, that the two had got a little tired of all the gossip. Jonathan Wilkes gave an interview in which he emphatically stated the two were not a couple. Robbie and Nicole both denied it, too. But Robbie was not above the continuing odd tease. Asked by GQ magazine to pick a list of Life's Rather Wonderful Things, he chose Nicole's scent as 'one part vanilla, three parts musk – the greatest scent in the world'.

Nicole was not the only woman Robbie singled out for praise in his list: he also mentioned his one-time girlfriend Tania Strecker, who had legs that went 'on and on … and on'. Other likes included 'women in cricket jumpers' and 'kissing with no agenda', adding, 'I love eight hours' solid shut-eye, with no nightmare that I murdered an ex-member of Take That or was chased by Stoke City fans. But few experiences beat falling asleep to "You're on Sky Sports with Rob McCaffrey!"'

He didn't stop there. Robbie listed steak and kidney pie, lamb kebabs, doughnuts and sashimi, as well as 'one of the final punk rock options available – peeing outdoors'. And finally: 'I like a cup of Earl Grey and a cigarette with a few of your best friends on the steps of your house in the wee small hours. The tinkle of gentle, undulating laughter in the soft, sodium light as we regale each other with stories of yore and vainly attempt to recount entire T'Pau lyrics.'

It was a charming little vignette and a perfect way to end the year – that and reaching the top of the charts with 'Somethin' Stupid', that is. And Robbie did appear to be winding down. He attended the premiere of *Nobody, Someday* wearing a Buddhist pendant, which had apparently been given to him by a Buddhist monk in Thailand. 'He called the teacher a great man,' said a friend. 'He's worn the pendant a lot since their talk.'

When 'Somethin' Stupid' finally reached Number 1, Robbie began dropping hints all over the place that he and Nicole were an item after all. Nicole was having none of it, perhaps annoyed by an incident in which Robbie had told an audience that Nicole was tired, adding, 'I wonder why.'

'Dating Robbie? Who said that?' she said. 'I'm also dating about five other people.' Asked if she had previously known about his bad reputation, she continued, 'No! I've had plenty of people tell me about it afterwards. He's actually very sweet and very shy and I'm very shy. So you have two very shy people. Was he predatory and pushy? Not at all. He was a perfect gentleman. Maybe I don't know enough about his reputation. But I take people at face value. He's been charming and good to me – and that's all.'

13

NEW YEAR, NEW ROBBIE

The year 2002 was to see some big changes in Robbie's life. The pressure of fame in the UK really was becoming too much for him to deal with, with the result that he was spending an increasing amount of time in the United States. Not for the first time, the irony was apparent: the fact that he had still not broken in the US was a cause for chagrin, but it also meant that Robbie still had one place in which he could be anonymous. It is a dilemma that has not been resolved to this day.

Even so, there was nothing new about the way Robbie kicked off the new year: by mooning when in the West London studio where *Top Of The Pops* is filmed. Dannii Minogue was also in situ and Robbie became rather jealous that she was receiving more attention than him, not least because she was wearing a see-through dress. 'If there's one thing Robbie can't stand, it's being overshadowed,' said a member of the audience. 'So when Dannii walked past in a see-through dress with her underwear on show, he wasn't going to be outdone. In one swift motion he'd slipped his trousers off his bum and bared all – much to the delighted whoops and cheers of the backstage crew.'

It was at around this time that Robbie was also involved in *Nobody Someday*, a documentary about his life filmed largely when he was on tour. The person who actually made the documentary, Brian Hill, recalled their first meeting: 'What struck me was that he was never on his own,' he said. 'I got to his flat and there were all these other people around him – security, PA and various other people. He saw me as another person who wanted a piece of him.

'He didn't know who I was or what I wanted. He turned to his PA in front of me and said, 'Why are we having a meeting about a documentary? There are always cameras following me around.' He hadn't even spoken to me at this point and he was saying all this right in my earshot. But when we spoke, I think he liked the fact that I was interested in the downside of what he does. He saw it as an opportunity to unburden himself.'

In the end, the two men got along famously, producing a documentary that really did show the downside of being the world's most famous pop star. And Brian was able to witness at first hand the fact that Robbie was winning his battle with drink and drugs. 'He didn't stop anyone from having a drink,' he said. 'But they were very strict about drug taking. Anybody caught using drugs would be sent home. He admitted he didn't know whether he would make it without relapsing. It is really difficult to go around Europe and get up on stage every night and stay sober and not take drugs. But he did it. Robbie was very strong about it. I never once heard him say, 'I could do with a drink,' or, 'I really want some drugs.' He was pleased that he kept clean.'

It was a major achievement and Robbie was determined that it would be a turning point in his life. And so it was that he finally decided to move to Los Angeles, to escape the kind of success that had comprehensively taken its toll. It was announced that he would take six months off and so, accompanied by the loyal Jonathan Wilkes, Robbie uprooted himself to LA, where he rented a £12,000-a-month, ranch-style house in the Hollywood Hills from the actor Dan Aykroyd. So content was he in his new surroundings that he cancelled an appearance at a Cannes music awards festival, where he was up for the award of Best International Male Artist. As it happened, George Michael won.

After a while, Jonathan returned to the UK to appear in *Godspell*, while Robbie continued to pursue a new life in the States, even deciding to stay away from the Brit Awards that year. But not everything was going entirely smoothly. In February the issues surrounding the lyrics of 'Jesus In A Camper Van' were finally resolved: Robbie, Guy Chambers and EMI were ordered to pay more than £250,000 to resolve royalties, costs and interest. The original song the lyrics were borrowed from turned out to be Woody Guthrie's 1961 offering, 'I Am The Way', as well as a later offering from Loudon Wainwright III. The judge, however, was extremely sympathetic to Robbie, saying, 'I have been in very grave doubt as to who actually won these proceedings,' adding that the copyright infringement was not 'cynical or flagrant'.

Robbie might have moved to the United States, but that certainly hadn't stopped him from looking for love. First he was seen out with the singer Alison Gunn, who had, bizarrely, been a Victoria Beckham lookalike in a Spice Girls tribute band called Nice 'n' Spicey. Then, however, Robbie was spotted in the company of a very different woman altogether. Her name was Rachel Hunter.

The first encounter between Robbie and Rachel, the estranged wife of Rod Stewart, came in a nightclub called 'Tangier', in which the two exchanged phone numbers. 'That's why I love LA,' said Robbie happily. 'There's a hot blonde on every corner – I never want to leave.' It was not, however, immediately to lead to a relationship. They had simply met and liked one another. That, for now, was that.

And Robbie was showing that he had lost none of his

self-deprecating sense of humour with the move. A video shown at the Brits when Robbie won Best British Male proved that. 'Hello Will from *Pop Idol*,' he announced from a perch by his swimming pool, as he waved his award in the air, 'You think you can take this away from me? Well, you can't. Three times I've won this, man, and you haven't got it. I'm much too strong for you. You want to take the food off my table? You want to stop my kids going to school? I don't think so. Craig [David] couldn't do it – what makes you think you can take it away from me?' And then: 'Good luck, mate. I think you're great.' Not that Robbie had any reason to feel insecure – he had by now won 13 Brit awards, more than twice as many as any other male star since the awards began 21 years previously.

Robbie did, however, manage to make one trip back to the UK: to see Jonathan's debut in Edinburgh in *Godspell*. The relationship between the two was stronger than ever. 'It's very special,' said Jonathan. 'We are like brothers. We've pulled each other out of loads of scrapes. He is one of the most talented writers in the business, which is very useful as he tells me when my songs are rubbish.'

Robbie was also on hand to advise him how to cope with all the more difficult issues that entertainers encounter, too. 'I had my first groupie experience,' Jonathan continued. 'I was so excited. I came out of *Richard & Judy* and there were 30 fans and the paparazzi. I was trying to be all cool, striking poses and signing cards. As soon as I got in the car I rang Rob and said, "Guess what?" And he said, "Yeah, you'll soon be bored of that, mate."' Indeed, Jonathan was about to settle down: he had just become engaged to Nikki Wheeler, a dancer.

On returning to California, Robbie added rather an unusual string to his bow: he became a priest, with a view to conducting the wedding of his friend Billy Morrison, a member of The Cult, to Jennifer Holliday. First asked to be best man, Robbie was able to up his participation after coming across the Universal Ministries church, a non-denominational organisation for which he was ordained online. On 1 March, he married the two at the Sunset Marquis Hotel and Villa, wearing, of course, a dog collar. Later in the proceedings he caught the bride's garter and wore it on his sleeve.

Billy and Jennifer were thrilled. 'It was a spur-of-the-moment decision and we managed to ordain Robbie, organise the trimmings and get married,' said Billy. 'The fact that my mate Robbie performed the ceremony means everything to me.'

Jonathan was highly amused by it all and brushed off suggestions that Robbie would conduct the event at his own forthcoming nuptials. 'He probably just got bored and thought, "I'm going to be a vicar for a day," because he can do that sort of thing,' he said. 'He does get bored, that lad. His mates in LA were getting married and Rob thought it would be fun to marry them. But he'll be fed up with the idea by the time I get married. He'll be by my side as my best man – and he'll have too much to do, what with his speech and organising my stag do.'

As for the man himself – 'Next time I'm in America, I may do a two-week intensive priesthood course,' he said.

In the background, however, trouble was looming from a direction no one had foreseen – Guy Chambers. Robbie and Guy had been working so well as a partnership that it seemed to have occurred to no one, including the two men themselves, that a rift between them could ever emerge – but it did. And the train of events, once begun, quickly ran out of all control.

The first intimation of trouble ahead was when it was announced that Guy was going to be working with Will Young – the same Will Young who Robbie had warned off at the Brit awards. That had only been in jest, of course, but this new development was too close for comfort. While Robbie might have been prepared to welcome his younger rival on to the stage, he had no desire at all to lose pole position – witness his behaviour after Dannii Minogue got more attention than him at *Top Of The Pops*, and she was no threat to him at all.

EMI wasn't too thrilled about this latest turn of events, and nor were they particularly happy about Robbie's new life generally, especially a new circle that also included Marilyn Manson and Ozzy Osbourne. It appeared that Robbie was becoming interested in a very different world, one that would not necessarily appeal to his existing fans.

'There is a genuine fear that Robbie is going down a very different road from the one that made him such a success,' said one insider at EMI. 'He has also started hanging out with Billy Morrison from The Cult and there are even rumours they have started playing together. It would surely be a disaster if he ever thought about going down that road – and I think he could kiss goodbye to his songwriting partnership with Guy Chambers.' These were prescient words indeed.

That said, EMI was determined to hang on to its star entertainer. Other record companies had let it be known that they would top any bid when Robbie's next record contract came up for renewal, while EMI itself did not have quite the clout in the States that it had elsewhere, providing further impetus for Robbie to look around. And he was clearly savouring the situation. 'We are doing the rounds of the record companies to see what each is offering,' said David Enthoven, Robbie's manager. 'The profile in America is certainly a consideration, but we're looking for the best deal overall. There is nothing more I can say as we're in the middle of the negotiating process.'

As the stakes rose in the background, another element of Robbie's life was beginning to come to the notice of the public. After that initial meeting with Rachel Hunter, it was becoming clear that the two got on very well indeed. In fact, they got on so well that it appeared they were now a couple. 'Rachel's the happiest she has been in years,' said a friend. 'She went through a very low patch earlier in the year, when she felt very depressed, isolated and lonely, but Robbie has changed that. The Rachel we're seeing now is brimming with confidence and is excited about her new relationship.'

As indeed were they both. It was not long before they were seen constantly in one another's company: bowling, watching baseball and going on dates. Robbie met Rachel's children, Renée and Liam. And he was prepared to talk about it himself: 'She's gorgeous and a great comfort to me,' he said. 'We've been through a lot and talk about anything and everything. We've been seeing each other for a while and we're there for each other through thick and thin.' The two were then pictured canoodling in the *News of the World*, in a set of pictures in which both started clothed and ended in a state of undress. Given that it emerged that they knew they were being watched, it caused an outcry. But despite the fuss, there were hopes that Robbie had finally met his match.

It was typical of Robbie that, shortly after the pictures emerged of him romping with Rachel, he managed to spark off a debate about his own sexuality again. This time he did it when he made a £10,000 donation, through his charity Give It Sum, to the North Staffordshire Lesbian, Gay and Bisexual switchboard.

But that item was quickly knocked off the newspapers when Robbie's ex, Nicole Appleton, published an autobiography, *Together*, with her sister Natalie. For the first time it revealed publicly that Nicole had had an abortion, a move which prompted Robbie to try to get in touch with her. This did not go down well with Nicole's beau, Liam Gallagher.

'Robbie's been trying to get hold of her at her home and on her mobile, but he's had no luck,' a friend revealed. 'Liam is more than annoyed about it and he has told Nicole in no uncertain tones that she has to fucking sort it out, and that he's not fucking happy about Robbie ringing his home. He's been ranting to everyone that, if he doesn't stop, he'll break his face. He yelled that Robbie's not the fucking FBI, he's a fat git from Stoke. Liam just gets mad whenever Nicole is linked to Robbie. It may have been over for a long time, but he doesn't want reminding that they were once an item.'

It was an upsetting reminder of a difficult time in the past. But Robbie's world was different now: he had found in LA an escape from all the pressures he faced back home, and he came across, on the whole, as much happier than before. 'For about six years, I've known that, for me to establish any kind of life without being under the microscope I'd have to leave England, and I haven't wanted to and it made me cry,' he said. 'I always used to think about the park that I went to when I was a kid, the walks we'd go on with the dogs, the picnics at Buxton – all those great things that I couldn't do any more. And I knew that I'd have to leave 'my England' which was the phrase that was in my head. England, as far as I can see it, is a nation at the moment governed by gossip and governed by what celebrity does on a day-to-day basis.'

His relationship with Rachel, which at this point was still going strong, was a consolation, too. So was his new record deal. Negotiations had been going on for months and finally came to a head in October. With Rachel by his side, Robbie flew back to London to sign a record-breaking deal: for a cool £80 million, some twice the £40 million that had originally been on offer. It was a staggering amount and made headlines as such: £10 million up front, £15 million on completion of the first album – *Escapology*, which had been recorded over the summer – and £55 million for the next three. In return EMI got a percentage of Robbie's merchandising, publishing rights and live performances, which made it a very unusual contract. 'I'm rich beyond my wildest dreams!' said Robbie with commendable understatement.

EMI had got its man, but even so it had taken a considerable gamble. Even an artist as popular as Robbie was not guaranteed to make back that whole amount and so a lot was riding on the new deal. But it had to be done. 'That was a deal that had to be made,' said Hooman Majd, a New York consultant who had worked with Island Records and Polygram. 'The entire music industry had been watching like hawks and ultimately EMI had no choice but to sign Williams whatever the cost.

'You can get away with a lot in this business, but let your biggest-selling act walk away and you're dead in the water. In the year since Alain Levy took over as EMI chief executive he had watched Michael Jackson's value disintegrate and had been forced to dump £19 million on paying off Mariah Carey's disastrous contract. Williams was the big thing he had left and with his investors watching and the competition circling, allowing the man to go would have been unthinkable.'

But it wasn't all rejoicing for Robbie: the deal created a huge expectation for him to live up to – on top of which, he had still not broken the States. 'I'm not saying that Robbie has plateaued, but he's certainly peaked and it's a question of where you go from there,' said Tim Abbot, Robbie's first manager as a solo act. And, indeed, with the timing that always seems to be a feature of any major announcement, a crisis made itself felt almost immediately. The simmering row with Guy Chambers finally came to a head – and the two split.

The timing couldn't have been worse. All eyes were on Robbie: having just signed one of the biggest deals in the music industry's history, observers were just waiting for a problem to raise its ugly head. And they certainly got that: the break was extremely acrimonious. And the reason was simple: Robbie wanted total commitment from everyone who worked with him to the extent that they wouldn't work with anyone else (the fact that Guy was working with Will Young clearly touched a nerve).

Guy, on the other hand, did want to collaborate with other people as well, and so refused to sign a deal that would have meant he worked with Robbie alone. Robbie was furious and released an immediate press statement: 'Robbie Williams wishes Guy Chambers the best of luck with his band The Licks.' The band in question were complete unknowns: Robbie was clearly making a point.

There were hurt feelings on both sides. 'Guy has decided to work with other people and on other projects,' said a spokesman, playing down the rift. 'After six years and five albums, he feels it is time to move on. *Escapology* is finished and Guy has co-written 12 of the 14 songs. He feels he is bowing out on a creative high.'

Behind the scenes, though, it was a different matter. 'The way Robbie has treated me is disgusting,' Guy fumed, as rumours circulated that Robbie had turned up at his house with an exclusivity contract and demanded he sign it. 'I've written five of his albums and he treats me like I'm nothing. It's a shame, because he's a great performer.'

The two were clearly both smarting. 'If it wasn't for him, Robbie would never have made it after Take That,' said a friend of Guy's. 'Robbie can't believe he has chosen an unknown girl band over him. Guy thinks Robbie's statement is full of sarcasm. But Guy is no mug and he has his own career, not just Robbie's, to think of. If Robbie is being sarcastic, it's a bit of a cheap shot considering the working relationship they once had.' It is safe to say EMI was appalled: the news went down so badly in the industry that its share price slipped. Robbie came in for some stick over his perceived arrogance, but there was nothing more to be done – the men had walked their separate ways.

It might have been the stress of the very public spat, coming so soon after the signing of his record deal, but Robbie now began lashing out on all sides, taking a pop at reality shows – 'I've nothing against anyone following their dreams – but not if they're crap' – before rounding on Nicole Appleton. Robbie had just been playing the song 'Sexed Up', which repeated the line, 'Why don't we break up?' 'The day I wrote this, I played it to my then girlfriend and I had closed my eyes to sing it,' he said. 'When I opened them again, she was curled up in a ball in the corner of the room – still, time heals all wounds. If you haven't worked out who she was, I dated her back in 1998 and she's now in a relationship with a singer in a rock band.' It was not Robbie at his most gentle.

In fact, Robbie was not in a gentle mood. 'I wrote this song last week,' he said, as he launched into one number. 'I wrote it. Me, me, me. Yes, it was me, me, me who wrote the song – and no one else.' Robbie might have had one of the world's biggest ever record deals, but he appeared to be in a foul mood.

Matters lightened up when he decided to include some swing numbers in his show and summoned the designer Nick Hart to dress him. Hart flew into LA. 'I was picked up from the airport in a convertible and, when we got to his home, I was taken straight up to his bedroom,' he said. 'He was lying on the bed strumming a guitar. There were cans of coke and ashtrays filled with cigarette butts all over the place. He looked up and said, 'I love your gear, man.' Robbie wanted some traditional elements from the past, and then to have me turn them on their head, which is exactly what I try to do.

'Rachel Hunter, his girlfriend, was there, looking drop-dead gorgeous. The whole scene was surprisingly unflashy and business-like. Everyone in his entourage had a job to do and got on with it. There was no alcohol or drugs. Robbie and I talked mainly about music. We both love Sinatra and I told him he should record his 'God Didn't Make Little Green Apples' – he seemed keen on the idea. Before I left I asked Robbie if he would talk to my six-year-old daughter on the telephone and he did.'

In November, *Escapology* was released and relieved everyone at EMI by going straight in at Number One. Shortly afterwards the single 'Feel' followed, accompanied by a video featuring Daryl Hannah, and while it didn't quite top the charts, it achieved a very commendable Number Four. Matters were helped further by *Escapology*'s position in the annual charts – despite its release in November, it still ranked as the highest selling album of the year.

By the end of 2003, Robbie had become a seriously wealthy man. At the beginning of the year, he had been ranked 962 in the *Sunday Times* Rich List: by the end of the year he had jumped to number 504 with an estimated £68 million in the bank – higher than George Michael. However, romantically he remained as troubled as ever. In January 2003, reports began to emerge that his relationship with Rachel was on the rocks, reports that were originally denied, until fresh stories came out to the effect that Rachel had dumped Robbie on the eve of his 29th birthday. Whatever the truth of it, they were certainly an item no more, with the split being blamed on Robbie's demanding personality.

'He is constantly fighting his own demons,' said one friend. 'It makes him a difficult person to be close to and Rachel couldn't cope with it anymore. He found it difficult being away from Rachel for long periods of time and hated them being apart. The relationship started going downhill, and Rachel just decided she needed a clean break. Rachel is a strong independent person and she feels she hasn't got room in her life at the moment for someone who is so needy and whose emotions are constantly swinging.'

A friend of Rachel's painted a rather revealing picture of the relationship. 'Some days he was all over her, saying how much he loved her, and at other times he didn't want to know and tried to dump her,' she said. 'She also found it difficult to be with someone who can't drink and spends much of his time playing backgammon.'

Robbie tackled the situation light-heartedly. 'I'm currently in the mode of looking for Mrs Williams, not Mrs Right Now, but I don't actually know a lot of people in LA,' he said. 'The LA culture isn't weird for me at all because I stopped drinking a while ago. It's great for me, there's a great coffee culture. So me and a couple of mates just go trawling around bars or the cinema. That's where Mrs Right Now comes by and says, "Hi." I'm currently like, "Free Single Pop Star, Straight Acting, Needs Wife."'

There was that hint about homosexuality again – although the time was fast approaching when Robbie would grow tired of the joke. However, just for now he continued to play along. Bearing in mind that gay men often call their partners 'cousin', Robbie related to gay magazine *The Advocate* in May 2003 that Boy George had come up to him and Jonathan at the previous Brit Awards and said, 'Hello Robbie. Hello cousin.' 'I look at Jonny and say, "You know what that means – he thinks we're gay." We always play at being gay. It's so tongue-in-cheek. It's funny people care so much. It's interesting to see how people get so ruffled up about it. We won't say either way what's going on at any time except we're best friends.' The fact that Jonathan was engaged, of course, made the real truth abundantly clear.

Life post-Rachel was also not all bliss. Robbie

discovered that some of the people he'd been hanging out with were not true friends and had faded away. 'They all disappeared very quickly,' said Robbie. 'You know all the things people say about Los Angeles and how it's flaky? Well, I didn't have my dickhead radar alert mounted, so I'm currently friendless in LA. I've just realised how difficult it is to trust people and it's put me on my ass.' Jonathan, of course, was spending most of his time in the UK, now touring with a production of the *Rocky Horror Show*.

Robbie continued to try to break the States: it didn't work. *Escapology* did not receive such rave reviews across the Atlantic as it did in Britain, with some critics claiming that Robbie's very Englishness worked against him, and that he should consider putting out an album aimed especially at a Stateside audience, rather than for the rest of the world. That did not go down well with the man himself.

'Americans have a great sense of the market. If they spent huge sums to put my album in the shops in the first place, it's not because it's a trial. They took into account what I have sold in the rest of the world and they decided to promote my album.' Even so, Robbie was treated very differently in the States from the way he was elsewhere: he appeared at a pre-Grammy awards performance in New York in front of a crowd that was waiting for the real attraction – Public Enemy.

But the rest of the world continued to love him and Robbie took his inability to crack the US market on the chin, not least by saying he didn't care. 'I don't think the album will break here, no,' he announced.

Did he really mind? Only Robbie really knew. But elsewhere his popularity continued to rocket, as did his career. Fears that he might have lost it after the split with Guy Chambers came to nothing: for Robbie and his fans, the show, as ever, was on the road. A great deal more excitement lay ahead.

14

AND THE BEAT
GOES ON

As time went on, Robbie's life continued to change
– and perhaps the biggest change of all came
about when Jonathan finally tied the knot in February
2004. Despite the years of rumour and speculation
surrounding their relationship, the truth was now clear:
they were simply extremely good friends. And so,
delighted as he was for his long-term chum, it was
inevitable that Jonathan's new matrimonial status
would cause an upheaval, no matter how happy, in
Robbie's lifestyle.

In the event, it was a day celebrated by everyone and,
very appropriately, not only was Robbie best man, but
the wedding took place in his home in Los Angeles.
'Robbie Williams and I have been best mates since we
were kids in Stoke-on-Trent,' says Jonathan. 'I always
knew that when I got married I'd ask Rob to do the
honours and he would have been furious if I hadn't.'

The venue was also perfect. 'We just wanted to get married, we hadn't a clue where – and then we thought about Rob's place,' Jonathan said. 'His house in Beverley Hills has the most beautiful meditation garden,' Nikki added. 'To get to it you have to cross this little bridge and it has its very own altar of trees. All we had to do was decorate it with fairy lights and flowers, and put floating candles in the pool. We wanted it to be very simple: beautiful but simple.'

'It was a fairytale setting,' agrees Jonathan. 'Nikki and I decided very early on that we wanted a small wedding. We really wanted it to be very intimate and special. It wasn't about having loads of guests: it was about us. We even wrote our own vows. We had all our favourite foods – lobster, steak and bread-and-butter pudding. Robbie made the most amazing speech. He hadn't prepared it, he just spoke straight from the heart – it was very moving. We got married at 4.30 pm and we were in our hotel room by 8.30 and asleep by ten. We were emotionally drained.' The honeymoon was spent in New York.

Jonathan and Nikki were clearly quite wildly happy with one another and conceded that their own contentment made them wish for something similar for their friend. 'I'd love Rob to find a girlfriend because he's at that stage where he would really like to be with someone,' Jonathan said. 'He was very happy for me and Nikki – and although I don't think our getting married is going to make him run out and do the same,

I think that when any of your friends marries it makes you look at your life. It's not easy for anyone to find true love. You can't just go out here and look for it, but at the same time it's not going to come to you sitting at home – that's the whole point of 'Love on a Saturday Night'. Sometimes it just takes time. And I know the right girl will come along for Robbie one day, just as Nikki came along for me.'

Of course, as Jonathan said, it wasn't easy for anyone, let alone a world famous pop star. Like all celebrities who have achieved his level of success, Robbie not only found it difficult to allow a relationship to develop away from the ever-present cameras, but he also found it very difficult meeting the right person. As he himself would allow, there are two different Robbies: Robbie the entertainer and Rob the person behind it all. The trick was to find someone interested in Rob the person, something that had not yet quite come about.

That year, Robbie turned thirty, a significant milestone. He had been in LA on the date of his actual birthday, but in March he invited fifty friends and family to an official party, which was celebrated in Skibo Castle in Scotland, where Madonna and Guy Ritchie had got married, and which was a restrained affair. 'We were all on milkshakes,' one of the guests, Max Beesley, revealed, while much of the three day stay was spent playing golf. Other guests included Ant and Dec. Robbie himself declared that he was in love with the scenery and wore a tweed jacket and deerstalker to blend in with the crowd. He appeared to take to the country lifestyle; forced to spend some time in Britain in order to prepare for the launch of a greatest hits album and his autobiography, Robbie chose not to stay in his Holland Park mansion, and rented a castle in Sussex instead.

But it was shortly after that that Robbie's past began to resurrect itself, demonstrating in the process quite how far he'd come. It had been nine years since Robbie had left Take That, and the band disintegrated shortly afterwards – remembered, it seemed, only for launching the solo career of one R. Williams. Now, however, it began to emerge that there was still real interest in the band – and, to the astonishment of all concerned, a real chance that they would re-form, albeit only briefly, at the end of the year. Interviews and a television special were planned, while the group and its members were welcomed back into the public eye as warmly as if they'd never been away.

There was intense interest in what the individual band members had been up to in the intervening years, but all that was overshadowed by one question: would Robbie be part of the reunion? In the years since leaving the band, there had been no end of barbed remarks about his former colleagues, especially Gary, and outright hostility to their former manager Nigel Martin-Smith.

It soon became clear that Robbie would participate in

some way, although it was the Robbie of the past, not the Robbie of today who would be on show. Old material was coming out again, and of course, it featured Robbie in the days before he left Take That. 'The band's record label BMG came to us with the idea of releasing live footage of their old concerts,' said Nigel. 'It was obvious that there's still a lot of interest in the band – and none of the footage has ever been put out. So we agreed to put out a live DVD – complete with Robbie. It will also coincide with the re-release of the band's digitally remastered back catalogue. The reunion is part of the deal. The lads are now deciding what to do but it will definitely include some TV appearances and interviews – and possibly a live special.'

But would Robbie take part? 'There's more chance of hell freezing over,' said the man himself. It was clear the bitterness still ran very deep. Over time, Robbie had come to forgive hurtful behaviour on the part of his fellow band members, and, later in the year, when the rest of the band reunited for a television special, he sent a video message apologizing for his hurtful comments and wishing them the best. He also had started to pay tribute to them at his concerts and had shared the stage with Mark for a rendition of 'Back For Good'. But he had not forgiven Nigel Martin-Smith, a situation that lasts to this day.

As the Take That reunion began to gather pace in the background, other rumblings were beginning to emerge, which would affect Robbie in the year that lay ahead. For a start, rumours began to surface that a special event was on the cards for the next year: a concert to celebrate the 20th anniversary of Live Aid. At this stage no one was quite sure what format it would take, but the biggest stars of the day were already being sounded out as to whether they'd consider being involved. In Robbie's case, as history was to relate, the answer was yes.

And he was also adding other strings to his bow. A film called *De-Lovely* was about to be released, a bio-pic of the great American composer Cole Porter, starring Kevin Kline and Ashley Judd. Robbie had a cameo role in it as a wedding singer and sang the song 'De-Lovely' himself, which so impressed the film's director Irwin Winkler that he forecast Robbie could have a future as a film star.

'He was so successful in this movie that when we do the TV slots to promote the film, we're using scenes of him singing "De-Lovely",' Irwin said. 'He's really great. I picked him for the film because I had seen a TV special and knew he could do it. Then I saw this photo of him with tattoos all over his body and he was kind of grungy looking but when I met him, I was surprised because he's a gentle guy. He came along to the studios and put on a tuxedo – which hid all his tattoos – and he looked great. I really want to use him again, I'd love to and I'm thinking of doing another musical. It would be such a joy.'

It was at this time that Robbie received a vote of

confidence from rather an unexpected quarter. He still hadn't broken America, and still veered between periods of intense ambition regarding the US, allied to a desire not to wreck the place that had become his refuge by becoming famous there too, when Britney Spears suddenly gave him a pat on the back. Asked which English singer she would want to collaborate with, she replied, 'Robbie Williams because he's hot and really sexy.' And if that were not enough, when asked why he had not yet made it in the States, she replied, 'You know what, I think he's just beginning. I think we should do something together and he'll blow up.' What Robbie felt about this was unknown.

But Britney wasn't the only one to praise him to the skies. His old school, no less, was also indebted to him when The Robert 'Robbie' Williams Performing Arts Suite was opened at St Margaret Ward Catholic School and Arts College in Tunstall by Conrad Bannon, its former head teacher. Robbie was not there in person, but his mother and sister were, to hear him being lauded to the skies. And, indeed, it was Robbie who made the opening of the suite possible: he had donated £50,000 to the school, which allowed it to gain specialist status as an arts college and thus get funding for the project.

'He was a super boy and it was great of him to stump up the cash,' said Robbie's former deputy head teacher Frank Jevons, who was then head of the art college. 'I remember him as someone who had a lot of flair and was made for the stage. He has been back a couple of times to see us and always comes unexpected. Hopefully, he can come again in the next few months.'

Robbie's mother told Jan of how Robbie came to make the donation: she had been speaking to Conrad Bannon, who told her that the school was trying to raise the cash. 'I spoke to Robert and he decided to donate the cash,' she said. 'Robert is very proud of his school and is always asking after it. He wants to know how everybody is, especially his old teachers and he keeps in touch with some of his old friends and Mr Bannon. He is hoping to visit the school soon. He wanted this building so it can be used by the children of the city.'

It was a fine gesture and one that demonstrated just how far he had come. Robbie had been famous for his entire adult life, but, with philanthropic gestures like this, he was taking one step further – into the pop aristocracy. He was becoming part of the establishment, someone who was far more than just a pop star. Robbie is still too young to be called a national institution, but that is clearly the direction in which he is now heading.

But, of course, there was still business to be done. The run up had begun to the release of his *Greatest Hits* album, which was due to feature songs from *Life Thru A Lens, I've Been Expecting You, Sing When You're Winning* and, of course, *Escapology,* as well as two new tracks entitled 'Radio' and 'Miss Understood'. The latter of those two songs was also due to feature in the second

Bridget Jones film, *The Edge of Reason* – Robbie had also sung on the first.

The majority of the songs were, of course, written in conjunction with Guy Chambers, who finally lifted the lid on what had really happened to cause the break up. 'There were a few reasons we fell out,' he said. 'We had been together for six years; we even went on holiday together. I think we got sick of each other's faces. But mainly he was about to sign this massive deal and the money had become so important to him. It definitely spoiled things. The deal became ridiculously huge and it became more about that than the album we were making at that time. I loved working with Robbie because he was so talented. We are not friends now and our parting was very acrimonious.'

In fact, Guy, who was now working with Kylie Minogue and Charlotte Church, looked back on it all with a certain degree of sadness. 'Robbie was a very moody character but I think that was what made him the star he was. I actually think that people who are very well balanced are not that creative,' he said. 'Our friendship ended very badly and we don't talk at all any more. People ask me if there's jealousy because I write a lot of the songs and yet he's the one who gets all the fame. Fame is a curse. I would hate to have photographers camped outside my house every day. I'm much happier being able to enjoy the freedom to play music.'

And Guy knew what he was talking about. Not only

had he witnessed it first-hand when he was with Robbie, but he had had a go at it himself and had no regrets about remaining in the shadows, rather than taking centre stage. 'I tried it myself when I was in a band called The Lemon Trees, but I soon realised that I didn't have what it takes to be a big star,' he said. 'People have to want to watch you, that wasn't me. When you meet Robbie you realise what true star quality is all about.'

And he still had happy memories of the time they were together, revealing that his favourite of Robbie's songs was 'Feel'. 'I remember we were out in LA on a songwriting trip and things were going very badly,' he said. 'He was at a real low point in his life and all the stuff we were working on was rubbish. Then one day I just came up with the melody for 'Feel'. Rob's lyrics came straight away because that was exactly where his head was at.'

Of course, possibly their most successful collaboration – indeed, one of the most successful collaborations ever – was 'Angels'. 'That was actually the second song we ever did together,' said Guy. 'I remember we'd just met and he came round to my house looking pretty rough. He'd been out of Take That for about a year and he was on a real low. He had the first verse and the lyrics for "Angels" and I finished the rest off. I knew it was special even then.' It was, of course, the making of Robbie, and in going public about what had happened, Guy might have been making a plea for his old friend to get in touch.

In autumn that year came the publication of *Feel*, an authorized glimpse into the court of King Robbie, by the journalist Chris Heath. The pages rippled with the sound of settling scores: Noel Gallagher, Nigel Martin-Smith and Gary Barlow were just some of the people to get blasted by Robbie who, amongst a good deal else, revealed that Gary used to charge his fellow Take That members £1 to use his mobile phone.

Robbie also revealed that the shots of him and Rachel Hunter were indeed staged, while taking the opportunity to have yet another go at Noel Gallagher, who had once so famously labelled him as 'the fat dancer from Take That.' Revenge was exceedingly sweet – Oasis had previously broken various musical records by holding two gigs at Knebworth, until Robbie trumped that by holding three.

And finally, for good measure, Robbie announced that he had never been in love. Indeed, the only real affection he'd ever felt, he said, was towards one Rachel Gilson, who he'd known from the old days in Stoke-On-Trent. She was the first, Robbie explained, and he still had feelings for her. Unfortunately, she had another boyfriend.

There were also signs that Robbie was beginning to get tired of some of the elements in his past, and that became increasingly clear when a newspaper published a story alleging gay trysts when he was a member of Take That. In the past Robbie had always laughed such stories off, but he had clearly finally had enough and decided to go to court. 'Robbie is absolutely livid,' said a friend. 'The story simply isn't true and he is sick of people questioning his sexuality. He's had a laugh in the past about fancying men but that's just Robbie on the wind-up. He is a red-blooded bloke and has been out with a string of stunning women. What more proof is there about his sexuality than that? Robbie is a good bloke and holds his hands up when stories written about him are true. But he is determined to stick up for himself when people spread lies about him.' The joke had clearly gone far enough. Robbie later received a substantial payout.

Robbie had also now found a new collaborator, whose identity caused some surprise in some quarters. The man in question was Stephen Duffy, himself an erstwhile pop star, who had been in Duran Duran before they became famous. He went on to have a brief solo career before forming the band The Lilac Time, which was influenced by folk music. The partnership was going to turn into a stunning success, but at the time it seemed a daring choice. Stephen was musically very different from Guy Chambers: Robbie was taking something of a risk.

In October 2004, Robbie made musical history. He became the first artist to release an album with video content on a mobile phone memory card when his *Greatest Hits* album came out, which meant that people with mobile phones were able to view his latest artistic endeavour on their handsets. The launch came about because Robbie's record label, EMI, had decided to work with Carphone Warehouse to sell memory cards that fitted into the back of mobile phones.

And the album was a staggering success. After its launch it went to number one in no fewer than 18 countries, prompting great excitement about the next album, Robbie's first with Stephen Duffy. They had 'established a very good writing partnership over the last year,' said Robbie's manager David Enthoven, adding that he had 'been privy to hearing the material and I know how good the songs are.' Of course, the pressure was on both Stephen and Robbie – Stephen to prove that he was as good as Guy and Robbie to prove that he didn't need Guy to be a success.

But still he couldn't resist controversy. Out on the publicity rounds to promote the new album, Robbie commented to gay lifestyle magazine *Attitude*, 'I've checked out swinging and dogging sites before. First you go in for a laugh, just to look, then you think, hmm, they're only round the corner. I've seen some very interesting stuff there.'

And, finally, Robbie appeared to have a woman on his arm once more. Although there had been the usual round of stories linking him to all and sundry, he had not actually had a steady girlfriend since splitting from Rachel Hunter two years previously. What happened, alas, is an illustration of quite how difficult it is for

Robbie to build any sort of relationship at all: the press and public latched on to this one almost immediately, which meant there wasn't really a chance from the start.

The lucky girl was Lisa Brash, a probation officer and single mother of two, who lived near Newcastle. The pair got together after meeting on the reality show *The Match*: it came about when a phone call came through to Lisa from a friend who had been at *The Match* and who told her, 'You won't believe who I'm sitting next to. Why don't you come over?'

Lisa did just that. 'Robbie walked right up to me, stuck out his hand and said, "Hi, I'm Robbie. I just watched you walk in here in jeans and a T-shirt and you turned every head in the room,"' she related of her arrival at the city's Malmaison hotel. 'Within an hour he had whisked me up to his room so we could spend time together in private. Once inside the room he said, "Downstairs you met Robbie...now meet Rob!"'

Initially it seemed that something might come of this, and Robbie invited his new friend to come and visit him in London, an invitation she accepted. Robbie commented that he had never seen the film 'Dirty Dancing', which gave Lisa an idea: after jetting down to London, she and Robbie spent the weekend together, during the course of which she entertained him with scenes from her favourite film.

'She said she couldn't resist the chance – after all, what do you give a man who has everything?' said a friend, to whom she had confided the story. 'So before she flew down to London to spend last weekend with Robbie, she bought the DVD. Robbie put it on his 50in TV and he must have loved it because he whisked her up and started doing the 'Dirty Dancing' moves. He was Patrick Swayze and she was Jennifer Grey. Robbie loved the 'Lift' scene where he raises her high into the air before she slides down his body. It's a very sexy move.'

The weekend was not without incident. The friend related that Lisa had troubles finding the loo, which sent her into a bit of a tizz. 'She hunted high and low but couldn't find the light switch in his bathroom and didn't want to wake him up, so she had to feel her way around,' he said. 'She was terrified that she might have peed in the bath or the bidet. But apart from that she is thrilled at how well the weekend went.

'She's listening to Robbie's CD all the time and is mooning around like a lovesick teenager. He's been begging her to fly out with her two children to see him in LA this weekend. He rang up her father and mother and they got on like a house on fire. Her mum runs a club and she cheekily asked if Robbie would be the star turn on New Year's Eve. Apparently he said "Yes!" There'll be a riot in South Shields if he turns up. He also spoke to Lisa's children and asked her six-year-old daughter, "It's Robbie Williams. Will you be my girlfriend?"'

Could it be magic? No. The relationship fell apart almost as quickly as it had begun. For a start, it turned out that she had previously had a relationship with Michael Mordew, a tycoon from Tyne and Wear, as well as dating Robbie, a past that led her own cousin, Julie Shaw, to sell her story to a newspaper, remarking that Lisa was a man-eater who had first fallen pregnant at 17, and that she liked to have a man with money. And if that were not enough, Lisa was also on the receiving end of abuse from fans.

'This last week has been hell – absolutely horrendous,' Lisa is said to have told her mother. 'I think he's great but it's ruined the life I had before. Sometimes I wish I'd never met Robbie.'

Then there was the fact that it was all so public. Hardly had the two met before details of what exactly they had got up to and when began appearing in the papers, not something that Robbie would have appreciated. To be dragged into a family feud between Lisa and her cousin didn't help either – and, after all, they had only just met.

Not that he was the only one suffering: Lisa had been having a miserable time, too. A friend told how difficult it had been. 'When she met him she was over the moon and told everyone it was a dream come true,' he said. 'But since the relationship has become public she has started to have second thoughts because of all the flak she's received. She was mortified when her cousin sold her story to a newspaper and basically called her a slapper. Obviously she was very hurt by the accusations and this has caused a massive rift. She's really not sure if she can handle this in the long term. She may go out to meet him and see if she can handle life in the spotlight – but she really doesn't know what to do.'

What she finally did was to sell her own story, too. It was obvious that the relationship with Robbie was not going to go anywhere, and so instead the reading public got to hear all about it. 'We've only had sex once – a fortnight ago at his Chelsea Harbour apartment,' Lisa rather breathlessly began. 'But he was fantastic in bed. He was all for me – not at all a selfish lover. I thought he probably was gay before I met him... but now I know he's definitely not!'

Robbie turned out to be the perfect gentleman and not just when it came to the bedroom – he knew what to do and say at other times, too. 'Robbie and I read the story which compared me to Rachel Hunter,' Lisa confided. 'There was a picture of Rachel in all her glory... and me. But Robbie told me the loveliest thing. He is incredibly close to his best friend Jonathan Wilkes, it's scary – but he said, "I swear on Jonny's life, I find you a lot more attractive than I ever found Rachel." He then told me, "Even though we've only had sex once, I've been thinking about having sex with you every five minutes since you arrived. I just didn't want you to think that this is what this weekend was all about."'

The first night in the hotel nothing happened, but the next day Robbie rang. 'That week he called every day,' Lisa recalled. 'Then he invited me to spend the weekend with him in Chelsea. On the Friday night we went to have dinner with Jonathan Wilkes and his wife Nikki at their home. The next night Rob's friend Dec – as in Ant and Dec – called and asked us out for a drink but I felt a bit overawed so we stayed in instead.

'We ordered a chicken curry take-away and played a Name That Tune game with his bodyguard. Next day Rob arranged for a car to take me home. He didn't want me to go. We were kissing and cuddling and he tried to make me stay another day. I couldn't because of the children.

'The last time I heard from him was last Saturday night. He sent me a text which said, "Be strong my supermum darling!" Rob knows where I am but he has no plans to join me in Orlando [where Lisa was holidaying] and I'm not going to be travelling on to LA. If I never hear from him again, I'll still cherish the time we had. I had a wonderful time. He's a wonderful guy. If he doesn't call I won't sit around waiting. I've got a great life.'

As for Robbie himself, he had plenty to ponder. The next year was going to be yet another eventful time: there was the release of his next album, he was by now committed to playing at Live 8, and there was the court case coming up. And there was still the old Robbie angst in evidence: he confessed to insomnia, self-doubt and any number of neuroses.

But, as ever, the British public just seemed to love him all the more. There are some people whose popularity is such that even their weaknesses and frailties become loveable. Princess Diana was one of these and Robbie is another. The more he fretted and revealed self-doubt, the more the public adored him. It was not, in many ways, a bad position to be in.

And there was something else coming up too: the big Take That reunion. Robbie sometimes showed signs of softening towards his old band mates and sometimes did not: Gary had come in for quite some stick in the recent book. And so would he turn up or wouldn't he? Robbie was playing his cards very close to his chest. And interest was growing. Take That was having a huge resurgence in popularity and so even without Robbie's subsequent fame, they would have been the subject of a good deal of affection. With Robbie, their phenomenally famous ex-member, they were set to hit the headlines again.

15

TAKE THAT

As speculation mounted about the Take That reunion, and whether the band's most famous ex-member would decide to show, Robbie found plenty of other things to occupy his time. Not only was there the new single and new album to attend to, but, as befits a member of the showbiz establishment, good works too. Like so many major stars, Robbie clearly felt that life had been so good to him that he should put something back, and he did so in spades.

Indeed, Robbie was now becoming notable for his appearances in aid of charity. By the end of 2004, he joined the ranks of showbusiness royalty, when he took part in a remake of the Band Aid classic single, 'Do They Know It's Christmas?' Recorded 20 years after the original, it also featured the likes of Sir Paul McCartney, Chris Martin, Justin Hawkins and Ms Dynamite and acted as a precursor to the really major charitable event in the showbiz calendar, due to take place next summer: Live 8.

But Robbie also had plenty to be getting on with before then: indeed, he was on a roll. Even more striking was his next appearance in the name of good works. David Walliams and Matt Lucas of 'Little Britain' fame managed to persuade Robbie to dress up as a woman to mark Red Nose Day in March 2005: their on screen characters Emily Howard and her friend Florence – two transvestites – run a dress shop which Robbie, looking for a branch of Burton's, runs in to. The two get him into a dress, at which point Robbie remarked, 'I feel comfortable with this. I feel like I've discovered the real me,' before skipping off down the street crying, 'I'm a laydee!'

But the occasion when he really came into his own took place in July 2005. The event was Live 8, also to mark the 20-year anniversary of Band Aid and Live Aid, and there was widespread agreement afterwards that Robbie had stolen the show. And it was quite a show to steal: his fellow entertainers included Sir Paul McCartney (again), Bob Geldof, U2, Madonna, Coldplay, Sir Elton John, Joss Stone and others too numerous to mention.

But Robbie rose above them all: he opened with Queen's 'We Will Rock You' – which brought to mind the scene-stealer of the 1986 show, Freddie Mercury – before launching into a string of hits and finally, in the middle of 'Angels', he went out into the crowd to sing. There was pandemonium: the audience lapped it up. Robbie ended as the hero of the day.

Indeed, his performance was talked about in some depth afterwards; no one denied that he had been the brightest star that day. One observer commented that only Robbie Williams could have played the crowd as he did: his unscripted walkabout was quite a risk, not only to Robbie as a person, but also to the performance as a whole.

But he carried it off and, more importantly still, the crowd's affection towards him was obvious. There was something of the little boy lost about him, still searching for love, and something of the entertainer *par excellence*, who could carry his audience in the palm of his hand. It was a magnificent performance and established once and for all how far he'd come.

But what about the music? A test of a different kind came in November that year, with the release of Robbie's latest album *Intensive Care*, which featured the hit single 'Tripping'. This was the first time Robbie's new partnership with Stephen had been put to the test, and Stephen had certainly done his all. He co-produced the record, helped to write the songs and even played some of the instruments. It was recorded in Robbie's Los Angeles home and on its release in November 2005, went straight to the top of the charts at No. 1. The relief all round – especially from EMI – was clear.

They'd done it: even without Guy Chambers, Robbie was a formidable force.

And Stephen himself had nothing but praise for his new collaborator. Although he had been a pop star himself, he had had nothing like Robbie's success, and seemed thrilled to be associated with such a big star. Indeed, he could hardly stop talking about the experience, which appeared to have been as rewarding personally as it was professionally.

'Recording in Robbie's studio in the bedroom of his house in Los Angeles was a thrill,' Stephen said. 'After a song you could step out onto the balcony and look down into the valley and at the hills. We have 60 songs which didn't even make it onto the album in the vaults and I can't imagine they'll stay there for long. Some of them are parts of songs which we didn't get around to finishing, but when we do the next album we'll probably start afresh because most of the songs on the album, like "Tripping" and "Make Me Pure", were written very quickly.'

Stephen seemed overwhelmed by his good fortune, but determined to bestow credit where it was due. '*Intensive Care* is the first time an album of mine has been in the Top 30, let alone the Top 10 or No.1,' he said. 'I co-wrote it and co-produced it but everything you hear on *Intensive Care* is really down to Robbie.' The message, again, was clear: it was Robbie who was the driving force behind the music and not anyone else.

The collaboration had been a long time in the making

and the real story as to how it came about began to emerge. Indeed, the earliest meeting had actually pre-dated Robbie's work with Guy Chambers. Happily for all concerned, Stephen had appeared on *Top Of The Pops* in 1996 to perform 'Me Me Me', with Alex James of Blur. It was a very fortuitous appearance. 'We bumped into each other in the *Top Of The Pops* studio and virtually straight away Robbie and I talked about writing together,' Stephen said. 'But soon after he and Guy Chambers became virtually the most successful songwriting partnership since Lennon and McCartney and we never did do anything.

'I didn't see the point in trying to get involved because they were so successful. But we'd still talk about it from time to time. Then eventually Robbie and Guy split up and we got round to writing together. We thought we were only going to write a song together and two and a half years later we ended up doing the whole album. There was no pressure. We knew we could take our time because Robbie had his *Greatest Hits* album coming out. It was all very relaxed.'

And Stephen painted a very different picture of Robbie from the one that usually does the rounds. He came across as an educated, intelligent man, far more knowledgeable than he is usually given credit for. 'Robbie quotes Gandhi on "Tripping" and he quotes St Augustus on "Make Me Pure" which I didn't realise until he told me afterwards,' Stephen said. 'He is a very intelligent guy and sometimes people don't give him full credit. He would come in and we would jam like a band. He would play the guitar and I would play the bass and we'd programme up some drums then we'd swap over halfway through. Or one of us would get on the keyboards and we'd work up an idea that he brought in.

'A lot of the Eighties' sounds on the album didn't come from me. They were Robbie's ideas, but people assume it's my influence. The album sounds like it was made by somebody who grew up listening to New Order, Joy Division and The Smiths and stuff like that. Obviously those are bands that I enjoyed, but I had no influence. It was the direction he wanted to take.

'When I released my last album, *Keep Going*, I felt that I had done what I wanted to do. So when he came along just after that I didn't have anything I needed to express through working with Rob, so I could just do what he wanted to do and I didn't need to chip in. He leads in everything. He is incredibly talented lyrically and melodically. The amazing thing about working with him was that he'd pick up the bass, having never really played it before: the first time he picked it up he wrote "Tripping". He basically sits down and comes up with hooks.' Again and again the message was being drummed in: Robbie's music is all down to Robbie! Although he might work with other people, it was Robbie who was behind it all.

But Robbie had not forgotten the other aspects of his life. He continued to do his bit: by November, he was more heavily engaged in charitable work than ever, and this time he was in the company of David Beckham. The two, both ambassadors for Unicef, combined forces to highlight a campaign to help children infected with Aids: they appeared in a video showing the two of them kicking a ball about as they discussed the dreadful problem.

'Robbie and I are proud to be involved in this campaign and hope others will want to unite with us to help children whose lives have been affected by HIV/AIDS,' said David. 'Even more shocking is that we can actually change this. Every single person can play a role in supporting Unicef's campaign to ensure children get the support they need to prevent HIV/AIDS from absolutely devastating their lives, as it has sadly done for so many millions.'

'Children are dying or losing their parents – suddenly it is children who are heading households, nursing their parents, bringing up siblings, dropping out of school and falling further into poverty,' added Robbie. He seemed determined to do his bit in whatever way he could.

It was not all good works, however. The Take That situation continued to excite, even if by now it was clear that Robbie would refuse to take part in an official reunion or concert, with a great deal of speculation as to what he would actually do. The concert was certainly not the only event planned: there was also a television documentary to be aired, in which, ultimately, Robbie did indeed participate. And one event, in which, alas, the fivesome did not take part in together, would certainly have added a greater poignancy to their regrouping.

As the end of 2005 approached, there was great excitement in some quarters as Sir Elton John prepared to celebrate his impending nuptials with David Furnish, once the new Civil Partnerships Act was in place. The idea had been that a reformed Take That, including Robbie, would perform at the party afterwards. Sir Elton and David were friends of Robbie's – indeed, they had helped him when he was in the throes of his drug addiction – and not to put too fine a point on it, the occasion would hark back to the band's earliest days when their fan base was largely gay. But the request was all to no avail. In the event Gary Barlow performed alone as Robbie refused to take part.

'Hopefully Robbie's snub won't upset Elton, who only recently forgave Robbie for claiming that Elton kidnapped him and forced him into rehab,' said a source. 'Gary was devastated that Robbie turned down a £5million offer to reunite with Take That for their forthcoming eleven-date tour. And he was hoping he could finally catch up with Robbie at the wedding, because he hasn't spoken to him since the band split a decade ago.'

Certainly, Gary himself seemed sorry that it had been so long since the two had met up. Given the acrimony of their parting, the rivalry and the bad feeling since then, it was heartening that both men now appeared to wish to put the past behind them. Time heals all wounds (except those inflicted by Nigel Martin-Smith, in Robbie's eyes at least) and it is possible Robbie and Gary were even beginning to look back with nostalgia on their days in the band.

'It's 10 years since I talked to Robbie,' said Gary. 'I've had messages from friends saying Robbie sends his love and is trying to get in touch. If he really wanted to reach out to me he could do. I know the day will come and I'm here when it does arrive.' It might, of course, have to be the other way around – that Gary seeks out Robbie – but the bad mouthing seemed largely to have died down.

And finally, as the year drew to a close, came the case everyone had been waiting for: when Robbie went to court over a series of stories that had appeared in a number of papers and magazines in 2004 claiming that he was secretly gay. Robbie himself, of course, had often joked about the rumours that he was more interested in men than women, but he obviously felt these stories had gone too far, not so much for depicting him as gay, as making him out to be a hypocrite and lying to fans.

In August 2004, *The People* newspaper had published an article claiming that he was actually trying to deceive the public over his sexual orientation at a time when a book about him, *Feel*, was about to be published. Robbie was livid. Clearly, enough was enough.

The case, when it came to court, was a sensation, not least because, once and for all, it definitively established that Robbie was straight, not gay. He had never given the appearance of minding all the speculation about his sexuality, but the upshot of this was that there were quite a few people, not least within the gay community, who thought he really was gay. This put every rumour, every whisper, every raised eyebrow, to rest.

And once Robbie's lawyer stood up in court, the gloves were off. 'Mr Williams is not, and never has been, homosexual,' said his counsel, Tom Williams QC. Williams went on to say that the paper alleged Robbie was 'pretending' that his only sexual relations had been with women whereas 'in reality he was a homosexual who had engaged in sordid homosexual encounters with strangers'.

Robbie won. The stories were quite clearly untrue and the case ended up with substantial libel damages being paid out, with the various papers and magazines fully accepting that the allegations were false. The rest of Fleet Street had a field day: there was extensive coverage of the case, which had stirred up immense interest across the country. Famous people's sex lives are a great source of fascination to the British public and to throw light into a few shadowy corners will always have celebrity watchers agog.

And it says something about people's ability to overlook the truth in order to concoct a story that Robbie should ever have been seriously perceived to be gay. After all, he had had a string of high profile relationships with a number of high profile women and never – not once – had he been seriously linked with any man. Certainly his relationship with Jonathan was an exceptionally close one, but given that the two had known one another all their lives, it was clearly a brotherly relationship rather than anything else. Besides, Jonathan was now married.

But it was a high risk strategy on Robbie's part. For a start, there was the fact that he himself had quite often joked that he was a homosexual, and so to go to court when someone else said the same thing (albeit seriously, and with the intention of making the fans believe Robbie had not been honest with them) could easily have backfired. In all the ensuing press coverage, there was a good deal about exactly that: all Robbie's quips were brought up again, all the times he announced he was about to come out, that he and Guy Chambers were a couple, that he may well have been gay but that he wasn't letting on.

And even more seriously, there was the effect it might have had on his career. More than a decade earlier Jason Donovan had sued *The Face* magazine for libel on exactly the same grounds, and while he won the case, many in show business believed it damaged his future. That was again another gamble that Robbie had to take.

The gay community themselves were split over whether Robbie should have sued or not. Peter Tatchell, the gay rights campaigner, was less than impressed. 'I am not Jewish, but if someone said I was, I would not dream of suing,' he said. 'Going to court over an allegation of homosexuality implies there is something shameful about being gay. People see the headlines, "I'm not gay", and conclude that Robbie thinks it's bad or shameful to be thought of as a gay man.' The entertainer Paul O'Grady (aka Lily Savage), however, took Robbie's side: 'I can understand Robbie getting upset.'

But the point, of course, was not so much about the allegations of homosexuality as those of hypocrisy, something Robbie made clear by his own actions. At the time that the piece appeared, he gave an extremely good natured interview to the October 2004 issue of *Attitude*. The interview was to mark the release of his *Greatest Hits* CD, but it did a good deal more than that: it gave Robbie the chance to make it clear quite how unconcerned he was to be thought gay.

He agreed to take part in a regular slot in the magazine called How Gay Are You: it was designed to test the gayness of the straight subject in question. Robbie went along with it enthusiastically, at one point whipping out a deodorant stick with 'rehydrating moisturiser'. 'How gay is that?' demanded Robbie. 'I am very nearly Donatella Versace. That's how gay I am!'

To make the point further, on the very day that he won the court case, Robbie also turned up on Australian television. 'I'm not gay in Australia,' he announced. 'I'm gay in a lot of places, but not there, for some reason.'

The case, and Robbie's refusal to take himself too seriously, had other unexpected outcomes, too. For a start, once and for all, it made it clear that Robbie was not gay. There had been speculation about his sexuality ever since the early days of Take That, not least because of the gay venues they played in and the very gay video they'd once made, speculation that Robbie himself had fuelled by the many announcements he made about imminently coming out. But here it was, finally clear: Robbie had been joking. He was not actually gay.

What he was, though, was confident enough in his sexuality to joke about it. Probably the only heterosexual megastar in Britain with a similarly relaxed attitude to it was David Beckham: while no one had ever accused him of being gay, Becks had publicly said how pleased he was to be a gay icon. Robbie looked as if he was going down a similar road.

Robbie then appeared on *Parkinson*, where he related what it is like to be a pop star. 'I had a few dates with this girl in America and it's like being Batman because she didn't know who I was – so she said,' he related. 'I believed her, she seemed to have a nice soul. Then I brought her back to my house and she looked around 'cause it is pantsdown palace! It really is.'

Indeed, it was a great deal more than that. Robbie had his own recording studio and much more besides. 'I've got a football pitch and I play about five times a week with a load of expats,' he said. 'We play three hours each night and we're a bunch of eight-year-olds running round with grins on our faces.'

But, alas, there was no time for romance. 'I've got to be realistic,' he said. 'I'm going on tour next year for five months. I just don't want to be in a relationship while I go on tour and nothing has really come along yet.'

And had he ever been in love? 'No, Parky. It's a sad, sad state of affairs,' said Robbie. 'No, not yet but there's plenty of time. I have all the time in the world.' This is a point of view that might have been disputed by at least one of his exes, but by now Robbie was clearly determined that there had been no really serious relationship in his life.

Of course, this stance might have been partly motivated by a desire to make a fresh start. Robbie's first serious girlfriend, Jacqui, had long since married and settled down. Nicole was living with Liam Gallagher and the two had a child. Rachel Hunter – well, who knows what really happened with Rachel Hunter and how the two of them felt about one another? What seems certain, though, is that Robbie had definitely had relationships he considered to be serious at the time and it was only afterwards that he perhaps came to change his point of view.

He did, however, display a certain amount of modesty about his achievements to date, saying that some years previously his record company had been on the verge of dropping him, but decided to give him one last chance with the single 'Angels'. 'Without that song I would not be here now,' Robbie said. 'If it was the present day I wouldn't have had the chance to put 'Angels' out because now you get two singles and then you're dropped. I'd had three or four. People have told me since that there were memos going around the record company, 'Let's drop him, let's drop him'. And then they decided to give it one last go with 'Angels'. I'm glad they did.'

That is entirely true. Robbie is a massively talented entertainer, but he was very lucky to create the kind of career after Take That that he did. The annals of showbiz history are littered with cautionary tales concerning former boy band members: it is not easy to forge a new career as an adult entertainer, and even less so if you develop the kind of drug habit Robbie had. He was also extremely fortunate that his record label were prepared to continue with him, even though he had not had immediate success as a solo singer, but he was also able to acknowledge this. Robbie might appear arrogant at times, but he still knows how felicitous he has been.

And to say his popularity was higher than ever is not overstating the case. Robbie was preparing an *Intensive Care* tour for 2006 and in December 2005, it was announced that Robbie would play at Croke Park in Belfast the following June: 80,000 seats went on sale at 8 am, and sold out within 20 minutes. 'It was a ticket lottery,' said a stunned Eamonn O'Connor, of

Ticketmaster Ireland. 'We could have sold out three Croke Parks and still not have satisfied demand.'

And, despite Robbie's continuing comments to the contrary, there continued to be speculation about a reunion with his erstwhile band mates. Take That had released a greatest hits album and had decided to form again to tour in 2006. There was widespread hope, among both the public and the other band members, that Robbie would join the line-up and tour with them the following year. It was not to be, and Lulu had the honour of sharing the billing instead. Take That and Lulu had worked together more than a decade previously and, in fact, it had been rumoured that she had had a relationship with Jason Orange, although that had never been confirmed or denied.

Lulu herself seemed remarkably upbeat about it all. 'We only confirmed I'd do the tour recently,' she said. 'I'm kind of big-headed – I sort of expected them to ask me. Gary Barlow said it was the third question they were asked when they held the press conference. I think the band must have thought, "We need that old bag Lulu on our tour." I don`t really know how they could have done that track without me.' As for whether Robbie would join in: 'Well you never know,' she said. 'I say: never say never. At the moment "Relight My Fire" will be the only one I will sing with them on the tour. But nothing has been set in stone.'

Even so, despite the fact that Robbie has continued to refuse to join his former band mates and, at the time of writing, looks unlikely to do so, there is now a sense that much of the bad feeling surrounding the break-up of the band has dissipated. All have spoken supportively about one another, and all seem more at ease with what happened to them in the past and the direction they are going in the future.

And it is fair to say that everyone involved had been damaged by the split: Robbie first and most obviously, but, as their profiles faded and they saw their former colleague's star begin to rise, the others suffered too. Many of those wounds have finally begun to fade away. And while Robbie looks set to be the most successful one for the enduring future, the others now have a career as a group again.

As for Robbie's own career, the signs look as promising as they ever did. Probably the most important test he has been through since splitting up with Guy was the reception accorded to *Intensive Care*, his first album with Stephen Duffy. All fears EMI might have had have been fully allayed. Not only was the album a critical success, rather more to the point, it sold well – very well.

And, traumatic as the split with Guy was, for Robbie it might have been a blessing in disguise. Had he become completely dependent on one man as his career progressed, it might have limited his development. As it is, Robbie has proven that he has what it takes, whoever he happens to be paired with.

And so, career-wise at least, Robbie looks set to remain in the stratosphere. He has matured into an all-round family entertainer, capable of appealing to every generation, and able to take his career to greater heights yet. Robbie has often played down claims that he wants to be an actor, and yet that is where he started as a child and he has already appeared in one film. More acting may yet be on the cards.

What certainly would appeal when he is older is to follow in the footsteps of his great idols – Frank Sinatra, Dean Martin and the crooners from the middle of the last century. He has already done an album and a concert singing the old great songs: it is entirely possible that Robbie may wish to devote a great deal more time to this in the future.

And of romance? That is trickier. Robbie continues to proclaim that he wishes to meet Miss Right, even as he continues carrying on with Miss Wrongs and, with touring a major part of his life for the immediate future, it is difficult to see how he is going to find the right woman with whom to settle down. And even if he does meet her, Robbie clearly still has what Americans call 'issues' in dealing with relationships. If his past is anything to go by, no sooner does he meet someone than he pushes her away.

But it is not uncommon for great entertainers to find it hard to settle down. After all, what can possibly equal the rush of euphoria that comes through a performance on the stage? Robbie is adored and fêted everywhere he goes, but nowhere more so than when he performs. He is undoubtedly Britain's greatest pop star, and looks set to continue to be so for the foreseeable future.

All the contradictions in his personality – his neediness wedded to his arrogance, his desire to break the States while at the same time needing it as a place to retreat, his desire for matrimony alongside his wish for freedom – simply add many layers to what makes up a much-loved star. The public has taken him to heart and there he is likely to stay.

And Robbie is, simply, an exceptional talent. He can hold a stage on his own, he continues to intrigue, fascinate and above all, entertain. There are currently very few really global talents on a stage full of mediocrities, but Robbie is one of them. The future looks almost certain to see many more twists and turns in what has been an extraordinary life so far. A global audience waits to see what will happen next.